THE WORLD ECONOMY

THE WORLD ECONOMY

GLOBAL TRADE POLICY 2011

Edited by
David Greenaway

A John Wiley & Sons, Ltd., Publication

This edition first published 2013
Originally published as Volume 34, Issue 12 of *The World Economy*
Chapters © 2013 The Authors
Editorial organization © 2013 Blackwell Publishing Ltd

Blackwell Publishing was acquired by John Wiley & Sons in February 2007. Blackwell's publishing program has been merged with Wiley's global Scientific, Technical, and Medical business to form Wiley-Blackwell.

Registered Office
John Wiley & Sons Ltd, The Atrium, Southern Gate, Chichester, West Sussex, PO19 8SQ, United Kingdom

Editorial Offices
350 Main Street, Malden, MA 02148-5020, USA
9600 Garsington Road, Oxford, OX4 2DQ, UK
The Atrium, Southern Gate, Chichester, West Sussex, PO19 8SQ, UK

For details of our global editorial offices, for customer services, and for information about how to apply for permission to reuse the copyright material in this book please see our website at www.wiley.com/wiley-blackwell.

The right of David Greenaway to be identified as the author of the editorial material in this work has been asserted in accordance with the UK Copyright, Designs and Patents Act 1988.

Library of Congress Cataloging-in-Publication Data

9781444367003 (paperback)

A catalogue record for this book is available from the British Library.

Cover design by Workhaus.

Set in 11 on 13 pt Times by Toppan Best-set Premedia Limited
Printed in Malaysia by Ho Printing (M) Sdn Bhd

1   2013

Contents

Notes on Contributors

Chad P. Bown	World Bank, Washington, DC
Maurizio Bussolo	World Bank, Washington, DC
Rafael De Hoyos	World Bank, Washington, DC
Camilla Jensen	University of Nottingham, Semenyih
Nasra Kara	Open University of Tanzania
Jai S. Mah	Ewha Womans University, Seoul
Denis Medvedev	World Bank, Washington, DC
John Alexander Nuetah	China Agricultural University, Beijing
Xin Xian	China Agricultural University, Beijing
Xianguo Yao	Zhejiang University, Hangzhou, China
Minghai Zhou	Zhejiang University, Hangzhou, China
Ting Zuo	China Agricultural University, Beijing

1

Trade Policy Review – Malaysia 2010

Camilla Jensen and Nasra Kara

1. INTRODUCTION

THE objective with this article is to give an academic analysis and assessment of the trade policy situation facing Malaysia. The starting point for the article is the recently completed WTO Trade Policy Review (WTO, 2010a).

Trade Policy Reviews are conducted on a regular basis for all WTO member countries and applicant countries. Malaysia became a member of the WTO on 1 January, 1995. The first review for Malaysia was conducted in 1993, the last in 2005 (Ramasamy and Yeung, 2007). The present review covers the subsequent five-year period 2005–10. The objective with the Trade Policy Review Mechanism launched back in 1988 is to enhance transparency in the area of trade policy by giving an objective overall assessment of the standing of each country's trade policy regime on a recurring basis *vis-à-vis* WTO objectives of achieving global free trade (WTO, 2010b).

The article is organised as follows. We start with an introductory note to the Malaysian context of economic policy. Then, in Section 3, we give a general analysis and overview of Malaysia's trading regime. A main theme of this section is the ambiguity of Malaysia's development situation. It is argued that several of the dual economy features may be reinforced by present trade-related policies. Despite this Malaysia has diversified her export base since independence. This is a major strength and adds an important element of flexibility in terms of future avenues for specialisation. In the remainder of the paper, we explore three of the areas that are treated as potential strengths or weaknesses of Malaysia's present trade and development policies by the WTO in the most recent Trade Policy Review document to demonstrate this point.

The World Economy: Global Trade Policy 2011, First Edition. Edited by David Greenaway.
Chapters © 2013 The Authors. Published © 2013 Blackwell Publishing Ltd.

In Section 4, foreign direct investment policies are reviewed. We discuss whether the present policies and recent changes in the investment regime have been able to recast the structure of costs and benefits of hosting FDI in Malaysia. Section 5 takes a focus on a particular priority sector for Malaysia, which is tourism. We discuss whether policies to promote tourism are wholehearted. What has Malaysia done to bridge dual structures in this sector? We discuss how the Malaysian government has been quite successful in approaching tourism combining a well-designed public policy framework with the dynamic mindset of private entrepreneurs. Section 6 focuses on Malaysia's external and regional trade partners and the combined challenges of competing in the Asian region under rapidly changing conditions. A short conclusion follows in Section 7.

2. AN INTRODUCTION TO MALAYSIAN ECONOMY AND POLITICS

To understand Malaysia's economy, a few points about the country have to be borne in mind. Malaysia is a very young nation having only recently embarked on the process of nation building. Prior to the establishment of the union of the Malaysian states (which includes the 11 states of Johor, Kedah, Kelantan, Malacca, Negeri Sembilan, Pahang, Perak, Perlis, Penang, Selangor and Terengganu on the Malaysian peninsula or what is called West Malaysia, the states of Sabah and Sarawak on the island of Borneo or what is called East Malaysia and the three federal territories of Kuala Lumpur, Labuan and Putrajaya), the area that today constitutes Malaysia has been under influence of several outside invading and/or trading nations. In terms of institutions, probably the British left the largest imprint because of the adoption of the Common Law system. However, this system of laws is not being adopted without challenge from other competing systems and influences. Historically, Malaysia has been under the influence of the Muslim world for the longest period in classical and modern times. This has left a colossal imprint on Malaysian culture and traditions. Minor influences are also seen from short periods of European settlements and from a short period of communist rule.

All these influences have left an economic system that can best be described as a mélange of what is today mainly a free market economy combined with a mix of oligarchic style and state ownership. Furthermore, the ethnic makeup of Malaysia also *de facto* means a large influence from major settlers groups from Asia – especially China and India – which are estimated to make up 30 and 10 per cent respectively of the population. Malaysia also continues to be a popular destination for settlers and international workers from around the Muslim world since it is one of the economically freest Muslim countries in the world (Miller and Holmes, 2011). Indigenous Malay people are estimated alone to constitute around half of the total population. The protection of the rightful interests of the

Malay people in the midst of all these outside pressures from what we could think of as ongoing globalisation has been an important factor towards informing economic policies in Malaysia since the 1970s and until today.

Major changes for the economy now and in the future will be more because of the influence that mainland China has directly and indirectly on the Malaysian economy. Whilst linking up to the new economic powerhouse of Asia, Malaysia is also under tremendous pressure of low skilled immigrants from very poor and/or politically unstable neighbouring countries. Few places in the world do we find a scenario of such drastically opposing development circumstances. Within a radius of less than 1,000 km, we can move from countries that count amongst the poorest (Laos, Cambodia and Myanmar) to countries that count amongst the richest (Brunei and Singapore) in the world. Malaysia is exactly the bridge of these very diverse levels of economic development (Hill and Menon, 2010). This situation places unprecedented demands and constraints on economic policies.

3. MALAYSIAN TRADE AND POLICY

The *de facto* trade regime in Malaysia may on the surface be characterised as highly liberal, because most instruments used are tariffs and the average incidence of tariffs is relatively low (WTO, 2010a). This is also corroborated by historical data from the WTO but administered by the World Bank as shown with Figure 1.

However, the indirect trade regime reigning in Malaysia must at the same time be classified as modestly to fairly discriminatory – if we focus on other policies that indirectly affect trade and drive a wedge between domestic and international prices (Menon, 2000; Woo, 2009). A number of such policies are in place today, the most obvious being those that affect different segments of the market for housing and cars (Malpezzi and Mayo, 1997, WTO, 2010a; Wad and Govindaraju, 2011). Indirectly a number of other markets are under similar influence such as the capital market because of the rebates or give-away shares offered to ethnic Malaysians (Woo, 2009). Another example is foreign-based banks that despite the recent reductions in requirements on ownership control operate under different rules compared with their domestic counterparts (WTO, 2010a, p. 58).

These markets function under government administered price discrimination schemes where sorting is sometimes by preferences (cars), sometimes by nationality (housing, banking) and sometimes by ethnicity (housing, investment). The practical implication of these policies is very similar to that of interventionist trade and/or investment policies. Their aim is to do away with dual economy features of the Malaysian economy, whereas in reality, they may be sustaining them. The most pronounced of these are the large differences between rural and urban, followed by differences between the foreign and domestic sectors. Both dimensions of the dual economy also have an ethnic component. These are policies that are

FIGURE 1
Average Import Tariff Rates and the Share of Tariff Lines with Peaks

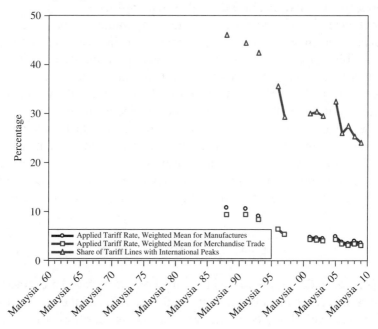

Source: The World Bank, *World Development Indicators*, downloadable at http://www.data.worldbank.org.

considered in the Trade Policy Review to be of particular concern in the context of trade in Malaysia today (WTO, 2010a).

Furthermore, the various types of instruments used combined with a lack of data availability from national statistical sources on important aspects, for example export processing zones or regional economic development data, make the trading regime nontransparent. This was also noted in the recent Trade Policy Review (WTO, 2010a). Similarly, Yusuf and Nabeshima's (2009) comparative work on Malaysia shows the great lack of knowledge about industries; either industry or firm level data or both are lacking to assess the real situation of competition in the country.

Despite the above, the trading regime of Malaysia is rated as amongst the freest in the world also by international rating houses such as the Heritage Foundation (see third column in Table 1). This is because the incidence of discriminatory policies is not *de jure* but only *de facto* related with Malaysia's external border.

One of the major strengths of the Malaysian economy obtained through its continued commitment to a strong export and outward orientation in its trading environment is the diversity of the export base. Malaysia shows very few traits of a natural resource-dependent developing country today. In 1960, more than 80 per

TABLE 1
Economic Freedoms in Malaysia

Year	Overall Score	Business Freedom	Trade Freedom	Government Spending	Investment Freedom	Property Rights	Freedom From Corruption
2011	66.3	69.7	78.7	79.2	45	50	45
2010	64.8	69.9	78.7	81.3	30	55	51
2009	64.6	70.8	78.2	81.4	40	50	51
2008	63.9	69.3	76.2	80.8	40	50	50
2007	63.8	67.6	76.8	78.9	40	50	51
2006	61.6	68.6	76.6	75.1	30	50	50
2005	61.9	70	75.8	75.3	30	50	52
2004	59.9	70	73.4	74.2	30	50	49
2003	61.1	70	73	82.9	30	50	50
2002	60.1	70	66.6	84.1	30	50	48
2001	60.2	70	66	85.5	30	50	51
2000	66	85	68.8	81.3	30	70	53
1999	68.9	85	72.2	84.7	50	70	50
1998	68.2	85	65	85.3	50	70	53
1997	66.8	85	55	83.6	50	70	53
1996	69.9	85	67	82.7	50	70	70
1995	71.9	85	67	78.3	70	70	70

Source: The Heritage Foundation, downloadable at http://www.heritage.org.

cent of Malaysia's export revenue is estimated to have accrued from natural resources as shown in Figure 2 using trade data compiled by the World Bank. Today that share has fallen to less than 20 per cent.

This shows that during the last thirty years, Malaysia has proven capable of spreading its export base towards a large variety of activities. In more recent times, there has been a rapid growth of trade in services, which today constitute around 30 per cent of total trade – well above the average for developing Europe. Whilst lacking separate series for education and health services, the available data on trade in services from the World Bank (Figure 3) show the composition of services trade on different sectors.

Financial and ICT-related service exports are minor but growing in importance, whereas travel and transport are amongst the dominant exports, which show the significance of the tourism sector to the present strength in services. Also health and education are not unimportant – estimated to be similar in significance to financial services. However, it is clear that at the moment Malaysia has a stronger revealed comparative advantage in basic services or the least knowledge-intensive types such as tourism and travel. According to the 10th Malaysia Plan (EPU, Chapter 2, p. 61, 2nd paragraph):

> The services sector is expected to remain the primary source of growth, driven mainly by the expansion in finance and business services, wholesale and retail trade, accommodation and restaurants as well as the transport and communications subsectors.

FIGURE 2
Trade in GDP, Terms of Trade and Structural Change in Trade

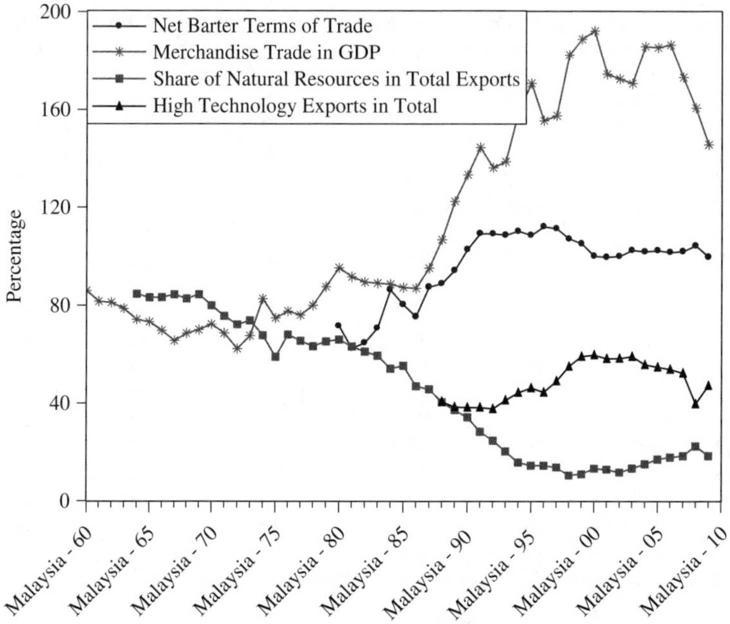

Source: The World Bank, *World Development Indicators*, downloadable at http://www.data.worldbank.org.

4. FOREIGN DIRECT INVESTMENT POLICIES

During the colonial period up until independence, Britain is believed to have been one of the largest investors alongside Japan and the United States. However, no data exist to verify this. Upon independence, foreign direct investment received less priority by the first Malaysian governments under Prime Ministers Tun Razak and Tun Hussein Onn. However, this changed and with the Investment Incentives Act of 1968 (Ramasamy, 2003), foreign direct investment along with trade started to receive greater priority. During this era, it was customary in the developing and socialist parts of the world (and this tradition continues to date in the Middle East and parts of Asia) to only invite in foreign investors under certain conditions. The first investment incentive act started an enduring tradition of discrimination between foreign and domestic held capital in Malaysia. Despite this differential and restrictive treatment of foreign investors, Malaysia has been able and especially successful during Prime Minister Mahathir's reign (1981–2003) to attract substantial FDI inflows (see Figure 4).

Foreign direct investors in Malaysia participate in production through three different types of entry modes that lead to various ownership constellations:

FIGURE 3
The Rise of Services

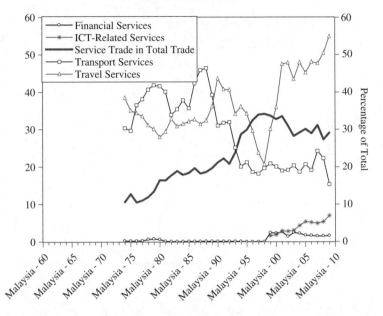

Source: The World Bank, *World Development Indicators*, downloadable at http://www.data.worldbank.org.

1. Greenfield investment or newly established fully foreign-owned subsidiaries which until recently was only the norm amongst small- and medium-sized enterprises and especially in trades or the least prioritised areas of the manufacturing sector.
2. Mergers and acquisitions in the free market which historically has made up only a minor share of FDI because of the restrictions investment policies place on this type of entry including the oligarchic nature of many of Malaysia's most important industries.
3. Joint ventures with local industrialists and/or the government (also called government-linked companies GLC). Until recently, the main share of FDI in Malaysia has been received in this form and especially in prioritised industries or in industries dominated by large market shares of local industrialists and/or the government.

However, the end of the Mahathir period and the Asian Financial Crisis also coincided with a new economic era in the world and especially in the perspective of developing Asian and European countries. Two factors have changed upon the entry into the twenty first century. One is the rise of China as an economic power that has a strong impact on both the European and Asian regions.

FIGURE 4
Foreign Direct Investment Trends

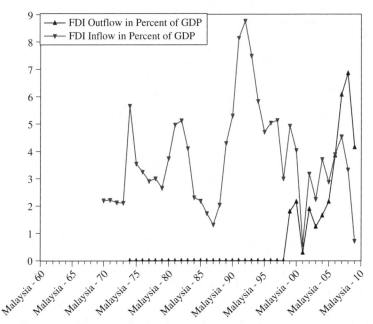

Source: The World Bank, *World Development Indicators*, downloadable at http://www.data.worldbank.org.

Potentially, this rise has both a trade and investment diverting and creating effect on Malaysia. How much diversion and creation that takes place *de facto* now depends a lot more than in the past on the conduct of policies in Malaysia. Second, with economic transition and new economic policies becoming the fashion, Malaysia is facing a lot more competition from neighbours that also try to attract FDI. The niche that Malaysia occupied in the past as unusually outward oriented, more developed, more skilled and English speaking compared with her neighbours whilst still very cost competitive is no longer as unique as it was 20 years ago.

These new circumstances have led to a new direction of policies in particular to foreign direct investment which we could call revisionist. There is awareness that the previous discriminatory policies may no longer be viable and that more liberalisation is necessary to maintain interest amongst foreign investors. Not least because of the vision of Malaysia graduating to become a high income economy by 2020 (EPU, 2010), that is based on resources such as skills and knowledge rather than natural resources or capital intensive industries. This has led to significant revisions of the joint venture laws, opening up of more sectors for Greenfield investment and fully foreign-owned subsidiaries (Rasiah and Govindaraju, 2011). The intention behind these changes is at least two-fold – to gear up again the inflow of FDI and to attract FDI into more skill and knowledge-intensive sectors. The 2020 vision of Malaysia is unlikely to be achieved without transfer of technologies from abroad that are not readily available from the 'shelf' to be purchased such as imports, royalties or licences. Furthermore, the red figures on Malaysia's technology balance of payments indicate that upgrading will be too expensive and perhaps also quite ineffective without participation of foreign capital.

This new direction for FDI policies may not lead to the desired results for at least three reasons (Figure 4). First, the changing laws are in a period of disarray – institutions may be changing, but the implementation and enforcement of new laws may take at least a decade to trickle down through the government system (O'Shannassy, 2011), that is, if the act in itself of implementing change does not receive greater priority by the government administration. The lack of freedom in terms of property rights and lack of freedom from corruption as reported with the Heritage Foundation's sub-indices (see Table 1) are in particular alarming from an investor perspective. These factors are more important for investors in the high value-added end of most industries and hence the type of investors that Malaysia now needs to attract. Second, the changes compared with other reforming economies of the last two decades are still modest and may not be as persuasive to potential foreign investors as they could be. Finally, the reforms may not be as effective as one could hope especially because of the lock-in created by established market shares, the oligarchic nature of many industries including quite restrictive investment laws when it comes to floating and thereby opening up for trading of existing Malaysian companies quoted on the stock exchange.

This new policy context can perhaps be better understood with data on annual foreign direct investment flows to (inflows) and from (outflows) Malaysia as shown in Figure 4. The recent downturn in FDI inflows, which notably has been accompanied by a significant rise in outflows, may have a number of different explanations that would confirm or affirm the hypothesis that the revisionist period so far has not been able to recast the cost and benefits of FDI in the way the government hopes – even though this may also be too early to evaluate.

The most popular explanation is that the decline in FDI has its roots in the financial crisis of the last decade and the more recent 2008 crisis. No doubt this has been an accompanying factor. However, it refutes the fact of the reverse and quite strong trend in outflows, which is a recent phenomenon. A somewhat competing explanation is that Malaysia's situation mirrors a capital flight scenario that has its roots in the general deterioration of the investment climate over the past two decades (Table 1 and Woo, 2009). However, this explanation is also

CAMILLA JENSEN AND NASRA KARA

FIGURE 5
Malaysian Investment Performance Compared, 2007

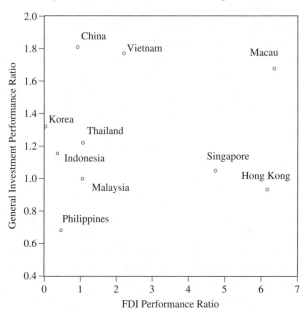

Source: The World Bank, *World Development Indicators*, downloadable at http://www.data.worldbank.org.

problematic in view to the fact that outward FDI is mainly in natural resource intensive industries and often undertaken by GLCs from Malaysia such as Petronas' investments in Africa (Rasiah and Govindaraju, 2011).

The most likely explanation is the rise of a number of competing destinations for FDI in the region (such as Vietnam). This is currently reducing inflows and also attracting some outflows from Malaysia even though they do not concern major government sponsored projects. For example, some Chinese–Malay investors are shifting their labour-intensive projects to Vietnam. Figure 5 shows a plot of the so-called FDI performance ratio as proposed by the UNCTAD team behind the *World Investment Report* UNCTAD, 2009). The data shown are for 2007, as the 2008 and 2009 data were deselected because of the impact of the financial crisis on the series. This index shows the extent to which an economy in successful in attracting FDI against the world average and weighted by the size of the economy. The same index was calculated for general investment performance, which turns out simply to be the investment rate divided with the global average investment rate. Countries that score low on both indices and hence lie close to the origin are global underperformers in generating overall investment and also therefore have difficulty attracting FDI – for example, more because of their general business climate than because of particular laws favouring or disfavouring foreign investors. Countries that lie along the y-axis are the independent investors that rely less on FDI flows. Most likely these countries apply strict controls on FDI but have a good investment climate otherwise. Countries that lie along the x-axis are the maturing economies that experience a levelling out of their capital build up but who rely extensively on FDI inflows and conduct open-door policies. Countries furthest out in the diagram are the best performers in terms of combining a good general investment climate with open-door policies.

A likely complementary explanation of the downturn is the shift towards an emphasis on services that are much less capital intensive in terms of investment per job or income generated. Another and also likely complementary explanation is that whereas the market in Malaysia for FDI perhaps is much less driven by free or open-market operations in terms of buying up existing companies, still the joint venture-based deals have their natural limitations as there is a limited amount of partners especially in oligopolistic industries. Finally, (and difficult to evaluate without additional information) is the role that the Economic Processing Zones played in the past towards generating FDI and today towards retaining FDI. At least the role of these zones seems *passé* or outplayed in terms of generating FDI into new sectors and activities such as service and knowledge-intensive value-added activities. It remains to be seen whether the revisionist policies to date are sufficient to realise the visions they entail.

5. TOURISM AS TRADE IN SERVICES

Tourism in Malaysia is one of youngest and fastest growing industries contributing positively to the trade balance. Mass arrivals have only taken place since the late 1990s (see Figure 6). In the very early days of independence, the tourism sector was not recognised as important to economic development. It was not until the mid-1960s that it became recognised as a vital sector. Malaysian governments during the 1970s decided to invest more by improving infrastructure networks for instance highways, airports, the condition of tourist attractions in each state, funding various tourism projects, creating peace and security and launching the first marketing and promotional activities.

To solidify the sector, the government also established several organs to make it perform to its fullest potential. These are the Tourism Development Corporation (TDC) and Ministry of Culture and Tourism (MCT). The success of the sector started to be recognised when the government developed the first National Tourism Policy (NTP) in 1992. Apart from NTP, other tourism-related policies were developed, amongst them the National Eco-tourism Plan of 1996, the Rural Tourism Master Plan of 2001 and currently the government has adopted the 2nd NTP that was established for the years 2003–10 (Hamzah, 2004).

CAMILLA JENSEN AND NASRA KARA

FIGURE 6
Tourism Arrivals and Receipts

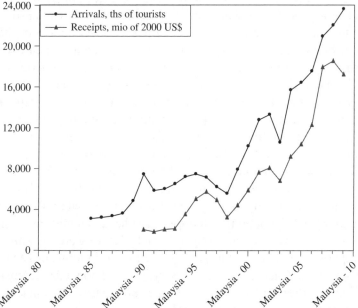

Source: The United Nation's World Tourism Organisation, *Tourism Factbook*, partially downloadable at http://www.unwto.org.

The tourism sector is subject to three forms of government and hence fairly decentralised in terms of decision-making powers. The Federal Government has the duty of overseeing all planning activities carried out by the Ministry of Culture Arts and Tourism (MOCAT) and collecting tourism revenues generated from these activities and subsequently channelling them back through an equitable scheme of tourism development towards all the states in Malaysia (Hamzah, 2004). Another major task of the Federal Government is to oversee and carry out marketing campaigns at the national level. The main responsibility of State Governments is to deal with formulating tourism development policies. The local authority or municipality is the lowest form of the government that has the task of actual planning, carrying out programmes and undertaking local marketing of the tourism sector.

The task of marketing and promoting Malaysia as a destination is left with the Malaysia Tourism Promotion Board (MTPB), a government organ that was established under the jurisdiction of Malaysia Tourism Promotion Board Act (1992). Malaysia has been using different promotional strategies to attract both domestic and international tourists.[1] The emphasis on the domestic segment of the market is relatively unusual for a country such as Malaysia and has received increasing priority over time with the realisation that the domestic market serves as an important stabiliser of the sector.

Today tourism is the second sector for generating foreign currency after the manufacturing industry. It is estimated that the contribution of tourism revenue to GDP in 2009 was 8.2 per cent (Tourism Malaysia, 2009). Because of the abundant tourist attractions, the World Tourism Organization ranked Malaysia as the third most popular tourist destination in the Asia Pacific in terms of generating more foreign visitors.

The increase in the number of visitor arrivals has gone hand in hand with a major increase in foreign exchange earnings from tourism. The global financial crisis merely led to a levelling out in receipts. By comparison, many other leading tourist destinations have experienced large drops in both arrivals and receipts in 2008 and 2009. Tourist arrivals from Asian countries in 2009 were reported to have increased the most by 31.5 per cent in Malaysia, whereas the non-Asian markets exhibited a negative growth of 1.5 per cent in the period 2008–09. In terms of employment generation, the sector is estimated by the World Travel and Tourism Council (WTTC, 2011) to contribute a total of RM 56.9 billion to the Malaysian economy equivalent to 7.2 per cent of total GDP in 2011. The sector is estimated to generate 768,000 direct jobs in 2011.

Apart from the international travel market, the domestic travel market has also started to perform very well. This market emerged after the Gulf war, bird flu and the Asian financial and economic crisis in the 1990s. After intensive promotional activities, Malays started travelling more frequently within their own country. Because of the limitations of observing domestic tourism activities without the frequent usage of surveys, the performance of the domestic market is perhaps best reflected by data on hotel occupancy rates. This is shown in Table 2. Occupancy rates reveal the relative size, importance and increase in the domestic market segment for the Malaysian tourism sector.

---

[1] Among these marketing strategies are the 'stay home', 'Malaysia truly Asia', 'Malaysia My second Home', 'Visit Malaysia 2007', 'Fabulous Food 1 Malaysia', 'Cuti-Cuti 1 Malaysia', 'Malaysia Mega Sales' and 'MyCEB'. Other promotional events used to market tourism are the Formula One Petronas Malaysia Grand Prix Championship and Le Tour De Langkawi (Tourism Malaysia, 2008). Apart from the above strategies other promotional campaigns used to market the sector are the use of sales mission and visits, the development of an overall affordable tourist package, participating into various local and international trade fairs for example Arab Travel Mart in Dubai, New Delhi, Berlin, Milan, Moscow, Australia and so forth, seminar and workshop participation, use of media (Newspaper, Television), online resources (e-newsletter, e-brochures, ministry's website information), etc. As a result of the intensive promotional marketing campaigns Malaysia's tourism sector has grown at an estimated annual rate of 5–7 per cent over the last 10–15 years.

CAMILLA JENSEN AND NASRA KARA

TABLE 2
Hotel occupancy rates by main market and state, 2007–09

State	Domestic (Share)	Foreign (Share)	State (Share)	Change 2007–09	Total 2009
Perlis	84.7	15.3	0	−1.7	102,547
Kedah	49.5	50.5	6	−7.5	3,846,529
Penang	50.0	49.9	9	7.5	5,960,329
Perak	78.2	21.7	6	1.8	2,523,029
Selangor	33.0	66.9	3	−12.7	2,839,229
Kuala Lumpur	42.1	57.8	20	−2.6	15,737,306
Putrajaya	44.6	55.3	0	3.2	181,104
Negeri Sembilan	66.3	33.7	3	−0.7	1,602,804
Melaka	46.9	53.1	5	8.1	3,759,515
Johor	54.7	45.3	6	−3.3	3,525,991
Pahang	61.4	38.5	18	15.5	9,652,909
Terengganu	85.3	14.6	3	2.2	1,219,127
Kelantan	89.9	10.0	2	−0.2	847,343
Sarawak	72.2	27.7	9	−4	3,908,815
Sabah	52.8	47.2	9	−6.5	5,362,270
Labuan	59.3	40.7	1	−6.6	294,549

Source: Tourism Malaysia (2009).

Over the last decade, the Malaysian government has successfully rebalanced the growth of the tourism sector towards a more sustainable pattern in the midst of international instability. That proved vital for the continued performance and survival of many establishments during the recent crisis. Even though the sector is performing well, it is also over capacitated in terms of number of hotel rooms and in particular in the federal territory of Kuala Lumpur. The data on occupancy rates help reveal this dimension. The dispersion of tourism activity is quite high, and the sector does not only have a significant impact on the more metropolitan and foreign dominated parts of the economy. Hence, we would rate it as one of the most successful sectors in Malaysia in terms of generating economic sustainability overall – that is securing simultaneously goals of growth, stability and equity.

6. TRADE PARTNERS YESTERDAY, TODAY, TOMORROW

For a country such as Malaysia, there is an ongoing discussion as to who are and should be the natural trading partners. As in many other developing and transition economies, the present day trade partners are not only dictated by 'natural' economic forces but also by history and established traditions and linkages. This being said, Malaysia today would appear to be rapidly converging onto a rather

TABLE 3
Trade Partners in Merchandise Trade and Tourism Services, 2009 (1999)

Partner Region/Country	Merchandise Trade		Tourism Services	
	Imports, %	Exports, %	Imports, %	Exports, %
ASEAN	25 (25)	26 (24)	61	80
Singapore	11 (14)	14 (17)	11	54
Thailand	6 (4)	5 (3)	26	6
Indonesia	5 ()	3 (1)	18	10
Vietnam	2 (0)	1 (0)	2	–
Philippines	1 (3)	1 (2)	1	2
Brunei	0 (0)	0 (0)	1	4
Asia	68 (63)	69 (56)	91	90
China (greater)	20 (11)	20 (12)	25	4
Japan	12 (21)	10 (12)	1	2
India	2 (1)	3 (2)	2	2
Australasia	2 (2)	4 (13)	3	2
European Union	12 (12)	11 (16)	7	5
Germany	4 (3)	3 (2)	–	–
France	2 (2)	1 (1)	–	–
United Kingdom	1 (2)	1 (4)	2	2
NAFTA	12 (18)	12 (23)	1	2
United States	11 (18)	11 (22)	1	–

Source: United Nations Conference on Trade and Development, UNCTADstat, downloadable at http://www.unctadstats.unctad.org and UNWTO World Tourism Factbook.

natural set of trading partners. In terms of merchandise trade, 70 per cent is within its own region – which is very similar to the within region trading frequency of other regions such as Europe (Hill and Menon, 2010).

China (including Hong Kong, Taiwan and Macau) and Singapore are the largest trading partners – where processing and distributive trades within and between the Chinese territories must be expected to continue to be the driving engine of Malaysian trade in the foreseeable future. Within Asia, the ASEAN neighbours constitute as a group, the second largest trading partner. Besides China and ASEAN, other important partners include Japan, Korea and Australasia. Outside Asia, the European Union and the US (NAFTA) contribute equally with around 11–12 per cent each. The rest of the world, including Latin America and Africa, are only minor trading partners. These figures are summarised in Table 3. When comparing 2009 data with that a decade ago (not available for services), we observe a quite rapid shift away from the Western Hemisphere towards Asia because of the rising importance of China and the Asian region as a whole. For Malaysian industries, this shift has not been unimportant and is perhaps one of the underlying factors behind the faltering levels of investment in particular in manufacturing (Woo, 2009).

In terms of service trade partners – where we rely on tourist arrivals from different countries as a proxy here – it is clear that proximity plays a much greater role for the development of this type of trade. According to these figures, Asia accounts for up to 90 per cent of all service exports, and the neighbouring ASEAN countries are dominant partners with 80 per cent of total exports. Necessarily, there is a bias in these figures because of the role of Singapore–Malaysia border trade. However, this bias may not be less important for merchandise trade because the Malaysian trade data are so heavily inflated by processing trade that does not involve a major value added component (see Maurer and Degain, 2010). Hence in a comparative perspective of the two types of trade, proximity does play a much greater role in services trade. This is of course not surprising because of the special characteristics of services and the fact that many are difficult to deliver over a great distance (e.g. they have to be consumed at the point of production and cannot be stored for later consumption). Similarly, whereas traditional trade with western countries is of the inter-industry type (EC, 2008), manufacturing trade with neighbouring countries is much more likely to have a great potential in intra-industry type of exchanges.

Hence, with the rise of China and the Asian region, there is a constant pressure on Malaysia to reorient and upgrade its trading patterns. With increasing competition follows a change in activities and with a change in activities follows also a change in who are the most important partner countries. With the shift of manufacturing industry towards China, there has been a great shift in processing and distributive kinds of trade. With the shift towards services in Malaysia and rising affluence, there has been an equal shift in particular towards making ASEAN countries much more attractive trading partners. This also shows how much a reorientation towards the domestic market makes sense for developing products, because domestic consumers are more representative of what the future main markets want and can afford. These trends must be expected to continue, and Malaysia should therefore try to make the most of trade agreements with these two important spheres of influence.

7. CONCLUDING REMARKS

Since independence, the Malaysian economy has developed rapidly towards a modern, free-trading nation that relies on a very varied composition of both manufactured exports and services trades involving a multiplicity of partners. Notable over the last decade is the rising importance of services where we have focused on a relatively labour-intensive service activity such as tourism as an example of one of the most successful industry cases over the last two decades. Another trend that may be of importance is the gravitation towards a much greater reliance on her own region for future trade developments. Overall, Malaysia has navigated very successfully under the guidance of the WTO to achieve a prominent status as one of the freest trading nations in the world today.

But whilst emphasising a liberalised trading regime, the government has paid less attention to the accompanying importance of liberalising the investment climate. The Trade Policy Review shows that the government since the beginning of the new millennium has taken significant steps in the area of foreign direct investment towards opening up for free, less regulated flows subject to a lesser degree of discriminatory measures in terms of distinguishing groups of investors such as those of domestic and foreign origin. However, we also discussed how these steps may be less successful in part because they do not go all the way towards abolishing all discriminatory measures and also there is a lack of targeting of general barriers and impediments to investment. Trade without investment makes little sense since investment paves the way for production and the value adding activities on the basis of which all gains from trade derive (Bhagwati, 2011).

At the same time, Malaysia should be praised for being a cautious reformer in times of great crisis, uncertainty and volatility. Despite the wellknown disadvantages of taking gradual steps according to the theory of second best, gradualism allows for constant learning and adjustment on the reform path. For gradualism and informed feedback to work, there is a greater need than ever for better data gathering and intelligence in Malaysia about the economy to inform policy makers. A great danger of gradualism that must also be avoided is that too little progress will be achieved – perhaps the essence of the problem of the middle income growth trap that many of the developing or emerging nations find themselves in today (Woo, 2009). Hence development and in particular investment policies may now be slowing too much behind the harsh realities of competing in the world economy. A good example is the free trade zones that might have worked well in the past but are not suitable instruments of development policy in a service and knowledge-based economy. The accompanying free-trade policies are in place, but to really work to full potential, they need to work in tandem with investment policy.

REFERENCES

Bhagwati, J. (2011), 'Why Free Trade Matters', commentary to the Project Syndicate series on *The Open Economy and its Enemies*, article is available at http://www.project-syndicate.org/commentary/bhagwati14/English (accessed 1 July 2011).

EC (2008), *Trade Sustainability Impact Assessment for the FTA between EU and ASEAN*, Phase I Global Analysis Report submitted by Centre for the advanced of Trade Integration and Facilitation and Centre for European Studies (Rotterdam: The European Commission, DG Trade).

EPU (2010), *Tenth Malaysia Plan 2011–15* (Malaysia: Economic Planning Unit, Government of Malaysia).

Hamzah, A. (2004), Policy and Planning of the Tourism Industry in Malaysia: *Policy and Planning of Tourism Product Development in Asian Countries*, Proceedings, 6th, ADRF General Meeting held in Bangkok, Thailand.

Hill, Hal and J. Menon (2010), 'ASEAN Economic Integration: Featurs, Fulfillments, Failures and the Future', *ADB Working Paper Series on Regional Economic Integration* (Manila: Asian Development Bank).

Malaysia Tourism Promotion Board Act (1992), *Laws of Malaysia 481* (Malaysia: The Commissioner of Law Revision, Government of Malaysia).

Malpezzi, S. and S. K. Mayo (1997), 'Getting Housing Incentives Right: A Case Study of the Effectiveness of Regulation, Taxes and Subsidies on the Housing Sector in Malaysia', *Land Economics*, **73**, 3, 372–91.

Maurer, A. and C. Degain (2010), 'Globalisation and Trade Flows: What You See is Not What You Get?' *Working Paper ERSD-2010-12* (Geneva: World Trade Organisation).

Menon, J. (2000), 'How Open is Malaysia? An Analysis of Trade, Capital and Labour Flows', *The World Economy*, **23**, 2, 235–55.

Miller, T. and K. R. Holmes (2011), *2011 Index of Economic Freedom* (Washington, DC: The Heritage Foundation).

O'Shannassy, M. (2011), 'Malaysia in 2010 – Between a Rock and a Hard Place', *Asian Survey*, **51**, 1, 173–85.

Ramasamy, B. (2003), 'FDI and Uncertainty: The Malaysian Case', *Journal of Asia Pacific Economy*, **8**, 1, 85–101.

Ramasamy, B. and M. Yeung (2007), 'Malaysia – Trade Policy Review 2006', *The World Economy*, **30**, 8, 1193–208.

Rasiah, R. and C. Govindaraju (2011), 'Inward FDI in Malaysia and Its Policy Context', in *Columbia FDI Profiles* (New York: Vale Columbia Center on Sustainable International Investment, Columbia University).

Tourism Malaysia (2008), *Annual Report of the Malaysia Tourism Promotional Board for the Year 2008* (Ministry of Tourism Malaysia), http://corporate.tourism.gov.my/images-/Annual%20 Report/Annual_Report_2008.pdf (accessed 28 October 2011).

Tourism Malaysia (2009), *Malaysia Tourism Key Performance Indicators* (Research Division, Ministry of Tourism Malaysia: Malaysia).

UNCTAD (2009), *World Investment Report – Transnational Corporations, Agricultural Production and Development*, United Nations Conference on Trade and Development, Geneva.

Wad, P. and C. Govindaraju (2011), 'Automotive Industry in Malaysia: An Assessment of Its Development', *International Journal of Automotive Technology and Management*, **11**, 2, 152–71.

Woo, W. T. (2009), 'Getting Malaysia Out of the Middle-Income Trap'. Available at SSRN: http:// ssrn.com/abstract=1534454 (3 August 2009).

WTO (2010a), *Trade Policy Review Malaysia 2010* (Geneva: The World Trade Organization).

WTO (2010b), 'Press Release, January 25 and 27, 2010, Trade Policy Review: Malaysia', http:// www.wto.org/english/tratop_e/tpr_e/-tp325_e.htm (May 2011).

WTTC (2011), *Travel and Tourism Economic Impact* (London: Malaysia Tourism Research, World Travel and Tourism Council) http://www.wttc.org/bin/file-/original_file/malaysia_report_2011-pdf.pdf (28 October 2011).

Yusuf, S. and K. Nabeshima (2009), *Tiger Economies under Threat – A Comparative Analysis of Malaysia's Industrial Propsects and Policy Options* (Washington, DC: The World Bank).

2

China's Economic and Trade Development: Imbalance to Equilibrium

Xianguo Yao and Minghai Zhou

1. INTRODUCTION

CHINA joined the World Trade Organization (WTO) 10 years ago. To open a window for understanding the economic and trade development of China, the WTO Secretariat seeks clarification from China on its trade policies and practices every two years. Since 2006, WTO has already released three issues of China Trade Policy Review (TPR) (WTO, 2006, 2008, 2010). Each tries to analyse the economic and trade development of China, report improvement in regime framework, practice measure and sector arrangement of China's trade policy and evaluate the implementation of China's WTO commitments during its report period. The most recent TPR was released at the end of May 2010, which covered all aspects of China's trade policies and practices between 2008 and 2009. The TPR confirmed the valuable role of China in resisting protectionist pressures and boosting global demand during the recent economic downturn, showed appreciation for China's stepped-up involvement in South–South trade and its duty-free scheme for imports from least-developed countries and acknowledged that China has continued the gradual liberalisation of its trade and investment regimes. The TPR also emphasised that economic restructuring and further trade liberalisation were keys to sustaining growth for China. Based on the TPR, this paper will also briefly review economic and trade developments during 2008–2011 and analyse the evolution of China's economic and trade policies in response to the global financial crisis. We will also evaluate China's achievement and potential problems in the

The World Economy: Global Trade Policy 2011, First Edition. Edited by David Greenaway.
Chapters © 2013 The Authors. Published © 2013 Blackwell Publishing Ltd.

recent economic and trade reform. The evaluation and comments also intend to respond to the doubts on China's economic and trade policies, which are commonly shared among western economists.

2. A SUCCESSFUL EXAMPLE IN COPING WITH THE GLOBAL FINANCIAL CRISIS

China's average annual GDP growth rate was about 10.5 per cent during 10 years since entry to the WTO in 2001. Two-digit growth has been realised for five consecutive years between 2003 and 2007. Most recently, China has succeeded in coping with the global financial crisis and achieved a rapid V-shaped recovery which rebounded to two-digit growth rate (10.3 per cent) in 2010. China's high and steady growth rate during the global economic downturn has attracted world's attention. The story behind China's miracle has become one of the major interests for scholars and policymakers from all over the world.[1] Not only has China stabilised its economy during this financial crisis, it has also contributed considerably to the recovery from economic recession of other countries. The importance of China's role in coping with the financial crisis is widely shared by economists at home and abroad.[2]

a. Economic and Trade Development in the Crisis

Although the financial crisis impacted on China's economic and trade development to some extent, the economic and trade data show China's resilience in coping the crisis. Figure 1 depicts GDP growth rate year-on-year on a quarterly basis during 2008–11. The negative impact of financial crisis has dragged down economic growth from 11.3 per cent to 6.6 per cent during first quarter of 2008 to first quarter of 2009. The economy has rebounded afterwards by boosting domestic demand and reached 11.9 per cent in the first quarter of 2010. What's more, the whole year of 2010 has reached two-digit growth rates, thus achieved a rapid V-shaped recovery.

China's trade was significantly affected. The sharp contraction of demand in traditional export markets led to negative year-on-year growth rate of export volume on a monthly basis. Figure 2 depicts the movement of China's export growth rate year-on-year on a monthly basis during 2008–11. The impacts of

---

[1] Not to mention to the most popular book about China miracle written by vice president of World Bank, Justin Yifu Lin two decades ago, another paper titled 'Grow Like China' has just been published on the American Economic Review in this February, which indicates the persist interests on China's economic growth miracles of western society.

[2] Nobel laureate Stiglitz (2011) considered China as being the pre-eminent case to provide evidence that Keynesian policies worked. In personal discussion with famous economists James Heckman and Richard Freeman in last year conferences, they all speak highly about the China's decisive policies in dealing with financial crisis.

FIGURE 1

GDP Growth Rate Year-on-year on a Quarterly Basis (2008–11)

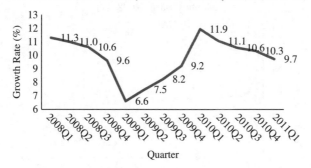

Source: Quarterly Database of National Bureau of Statistics (NBS).

FIGURE 2

Export Growth Rate Year-on-year on a Monthly Basis (2008–11)

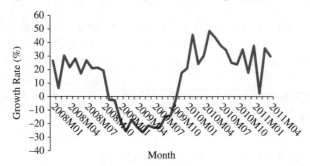

Source: Monthly Database of China Customs.

financial crisis on the export sector are more severe and persistent, but export volume recovered to its pre-crisis level by the end of 2009. The export recovery remains in 2010 to form a U-shaped trajectory.

Meanwhile, the global financial crisis also had a significant impact on China's foreign direct investment (FDI). From Figure 3, it can be seen that the monthly growth rate of FDI dropped dramatically from 109.8 per cent to −32.7 per cent during first quarter of 2008 to first quarter of 2009. Both external and internal factors account for this decrease. First, the financial constraints for multinational corporations in the originating countries make it harder for them to invest in China. Second, the foreign invested enterprises (FIEs), which take half of China's trade,[3] were less willing and able to make additional investment because of the sharp

---

[3] In 2009, the share of FIEs engaging export has reached 55.2 per cent, where the export share is 59.9 per cent, and the import share is 54.2 per cent (National Bureau of Statistics, 2010). Meanwhile, the FIEs also account for around 84 per cent of its processing trade (WTO, 2010).

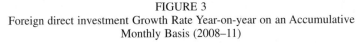

FIGURE 3
Foreign direct investment Growth Rate Year-on-year on an Accumulative
Monthly Basis (2008–11)

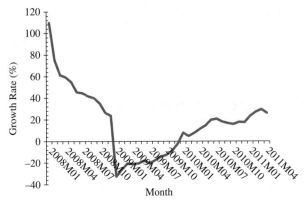

Source: Monthly Database of Ministry of Commerce (MOFCOM).

contraction of external demand. The growth rate of FDI increased significantly after 2009. However, the lack of momentum has formed an inclined V-shaped growth curve. This also implies that the recovery of other countries is much slower than that of China.

In all, China showed great resilience in the face of the sharp decline in external demand, largely because of expansionary fiscal and monetary policies.

b. Outstanding Performance During the Crisis

China can be considered as a shining star in coping with financial crisis. Table 1 compares China's GDP accounts with other countries and regions from the first quarter of 2008 to the first quarter of 2011. We find that China's economic performance has far surpassed other countries and regions. GDP growth surpassed United States by 9.56 per cent, the United Kingdom by 10.81 per cent and it is also much higher than another key emerging economy Brazil by 4.77 per cent. Even for the export sector most affected, the quarterly average growth rate is the fastest around the world at 12.53 per cent. The highest growth rate of investment of China not only contributes most for the whole economy, but also indicates the efficacy of its stimulus policies. The cross-country comparison shows that emerging economies such as China, Korea and Brazil have recovered quickly. Meanwhile, industrialised countries either show signs of recovery with zero economic growth (e.g. United States and Germany) or are still in the grip of the crisis with negative growth rates (e.g. France, United Kingdom and Japan). When the global financial crisis still grinds on for the western world, China's economic stability and high growth is really important to the health of the global economy.

TABLE 1

Cross-Countries Comparison of GDP Growth Accounts (2008 Q1 to 2011 Q1)

Country/accounts	GDP	Investment	Consumption	Export	Import
China	9.82	27.96	18.60	12.53	18.59
Brazil	4.05	5.64	5.64	−4.27	13.61
Korea	3.05	1.94	1.94	7.60	5.28
Russian Federation	0.56	2.88	2.88	1.36	2.66
United States	0.26	0.30	0.30	3.28	−0.37
Germany	0.24	0.45	0.45	1.70	2.79
France	−0.27	0.68	0.68	−0.49	0.26
United Kingdom	−0.99	−0.70	−0.70	−0.33	−0.99
Japan	−1.10	−0.32	−0.32	1.56	−0.91
OECD	0.11	0.25	0.25	0.92	−0.09
G7	−0.19	0.08	0.08	0.04	−0.66
EU(27)	−0.42	−0.06	−0.06	−0.15	−0.60
Euro Area (17)	−0.44	0.02	0.02	−0.40	−0.66

Source: All data are year-on-year growth rate on a quarterly basis from the first quarter of 2008 to the first quarter of 2011; China's data are from NBS, China Customs and MOFCOM, and the quarterly data of investment, consumption, export and import are aggregated through monthly data by authors' calculation; Data of other countries and regions are from OECD statistical database http://stats.oecd.org/Index.aspx, where data of the first quarter of 2011 for Russia and Brazil, and all organisations are not available. Because of limitation of Chinese data, the urban fixed asset investment is proxy for capital formation, and total retail sales of consumer goods are proxy for consumption which may cause comparable issues with other countries.

TABLE 2

Changes in Ranking of China in the World before and after Crisis

Item/ranking	Before crisis (2007)	After crisis (2010)
Gross domestic product	4	2
Total value of trade	3	2
Total value of exports	2	1
Total value of imports	3	2
Foreign Direct investment	6	2
Exchange reserve	1	1

Source: Data of 2007 are from *International Statistical Yearbook 2010*; Data of 2010 are obtained by authors' calculation by combing and comparing data from IMF, UNCTAD, NBS, China Customs and MOFCOM.

China's outstanding performance has also significantly improved its international standing. Table 2 denotes changes in ranking of China's main economic indicators before and after the crisis.[4] China has consecutively overtaken Germany and Japan to become the second largest economy after United States. In 2009, the

---

[4] Generally speaking, the outbreak of this global financial crisis can be marked as bankruptcy of Lehman Brothers on 15 September, 2008. Therefore, the paper takes year 2007 as before crisis. There is no final settlement on whether the financial crisis has finished or not. We denote year 2010 as after the crisis, although it does not automatically mean the crisis is over.

total trade volume of China reached to US$1 billion and ranked second after the crisis. China also ranked second largest importer and overtook Germany to become the world largest exporter. China enjoyed a dramatic rise in ranks in terms of FDI volume, up from sixth to second. Thus, it became the second largest recipient of FDI after the United States, and largest recipient of FDI among developing countries. The rising international standing indicates that China plays a more important role in the international division of labour and has increasing impacts on the global economy.

c. Effects of Financial Crisis on the Evolution of Trade Polices

Although the global financial crisis imposed great pressures on China's economy, its overall trade policy aim has remained unchanged since its previous TPR. China devotes itself to accelerating the opening of its economy to the outside world, introducing foreign technology, developing foreign trade and promoting economic development that is 'mutually beneficial' with its trading partners.[5] For example, China has been participating actively in the Doha Development Agenda negotiations. It grants at least MFN treatment to most WTO Members, enforces China–New Zealand and China–Singapore free trade agreements (FTA) and implements China–Pakistan FTA on Trade in Services and China–ASEAN FTA on Investment. China has considerably reduced its tariffs and other barriers to imports. Its simple average applied MFN tariff rate was cut from around 50 per cent in the early 1980s to 15.6 per cent in 2001 and to 9.5 per cent in 2009, which resisted a protectionist response to the effects of the global economic recession. The MFN bound rates are close to the applied rates, giving the tariff a high degree of predictability. Therefore, China is the only major economy that registered an increase in imports during the crisis (WTO, 2010).[6]

China has continued to adopt measures to increase the transparency of its trade and trade-related policies, practices and measures. During 2008–11, it has adopted several new or revised trade-related laws, including the Anti-Monopoly Law, the Enterprise Income Tax Law, the Patent Law and the Provisions on Disclosure of Government Information. The Anti-Monopoly Law and Patent Law received approval from WTO members. By reinforcing the protection of intellectual property, the two laws will greatly promote the willingness and ability of Chinese enterprises to innovate. The reform of its tax system makes it more neutral and fair in forming a fair market environment which involves the unification of

---

[5] This argument can be confirmed by individual observer. For example, Branstetter and Lardy (2008) review the developments in Chinese trade and investment since the reform and opening up and argue that China's adoption of one of the world's most open trade and FDI regimes stands is one of the most significant accomplishments of the reform era.

[6] According to the WTO, at a time when world trade declined by 12.9 per cent, China maintained an import growth of 2.8 per cent.

enterprise income tax rates for all companies, both domestic and foreign and the transformation of VAT from a production-based to a consumption-based tax. Last but not least, the Provisions on Disclosure of Government Information increased the transparency of government policies.

Since its previous review, China has relaxed restrictions on FDI in services, notably in telecommunications, tourism and finance.[7] Also, the central government has been delegating licensing authority to local governments for the establishment and modification of operations of 'encouraged' FIEs and certain selected sectors, as well as certain types of FIEs, such as foreign invested joint-stock companies. It should be noted that the opening policy for services sectors is one of the major spotlights in recent achievements.

All in all, the liberal view of China's trade policies has created huge exporting market for its trading partners, thus helping the global economy to recovery from crisis as soon as possible.

3. IMBALANCE ISSUES EXPOSED DURING THE CRISIS

Nevertheless, many potential problems were exposed by the financial crisis. These problems mainly indicate two unbalanced features of China's economic operation system, namely international and domestic imbalance.

a. International Imbalance: Games with No Winner

The most prominent feature of international imbalance is large current account and exchange reserves, resulting mainly from the large and persistent trade surplus between China and industrialised countries (notably EU and United States). Table 3 shows that the current account surplus has reached more than 10 per cent of GDP, and the trade surplus 9 per cent of GDP. Some western economists concerned about the long-term trade imbalance between China and other developed countries argue that China's embrace of globalisation has lowered the wages of blue-collar workers in the United States and 'stolen' job opportunities of unskilled workers in Europe (Bertola and Ichino, 1995; Freeman, 1995; Sachs and Shatz, 1996). What is more, China is even considered to blame for the global financial crisis.[8] Although the accusations seem to be an excuse for transferring domestic pressures

---

[7] Here, finance sector mainly refers to banks, insurance and electronic payment systems.

[8] Former US Treasury Secretary Henry Paulson and Federal Reserve chairman Ben Bernanke also shared similar views that super-abundant savings from fast-growing emerging nations such as China put downward pressure on risks and laid the seeds of a global credit bubble that extended far beyond the US sub-prime mortgage market and has now burst with devastating consequences worldwide (Guha, 2009).

TABLE 3
China's International Balance Sheet 2005–10 (Per Cent of GDP)

External sector/year	2005	2006	2007	2008	2009	2010
Current account balance	7.1	9.2	10.6	9.4	6.1	5.2
Net merchandise trade	5.9	8.0	9.0	8.0	5.1	4.3
Value of exports	33.8	35.7	34.9	31.7	24.5	26.9
Value of imports	27.8	27.7	25.9	23.8	19.4	23.8
Services trade balance	−0.4	−0.3	−0.2	−0.3	−0.6	−0.4
Capital account	0.2	0.1	0.1	0.1	0.1	0.1
Financial account	2.6	0.2	2.0	0.4	2.9	3.8
Foreign direct investment	3.0	2.2	3.5	2.1	0.7	3.2
Balance-of-payments	9.2	9.1	13.2	9.3	8.1	8.1
Foreign exchange (US$ billion; end period)	818.9	1066.3	1528.2	1946.0	2399.2	2847.3

Source: Data from 2005 to 2009 are from corresponding years of *China Statistical Yearbook*; International balance data of 2010 are obtained from State Foreign Exchange Administration. The import and export data of 2010 are drawn from 2010 *Statistical Communiqué on the National Economic and Social Development*, therefore, the net merchandise trade share is different from subtracting export share with import share because of different statistical calibre.

of industrialised countries, they also imply that the western labour markets are experiencing shocks from the globalisation process of emerging economies.

In fact, the pattern of 'China's Manufacturing and Global Consuming' does not greatly benefit China itself. As China's exports concentrate on low value-added and labour intensive products, large trade surpluses do not bring high profit rates for Chinese enterprises, and Chinese workers do not experience rapid income growth. The trade surplus has been transferred into a high volume of exchange reserve. China's reserves increased 3.5-fold during 2005–10 and reached US$3 trillion at the end of March 2011. The reserves have been heavily invested in US government bonds with a low rate of return. This investment portfolio has turned into a leaking bag of rice. Therefore, maintaining and increasing the value of the exchange rate becomes a hot topic for Chinese scholars. The large-scale holdings of government bonds help lower the inflation rate of United States, and these 'Chinese Dollars' go back to China seeking high rate of return by hedge fund and equity investment. This forms what Stiglitz called 'Capital Doubtful Recycling' and brings imported inflation in China. The Chinese government sought ways to best utilise the large foreign exchange reserve; however, the discussion about using US$3 trillion reserve indicates the dilemma caused by the imbalance feature of international balance sheet.

b. Domestic Imbalance: Growth without Enriching People

Domestic imbalance can be shown as slow income growth and labour's decreasing share in national income. Table 4 shows that income growth of urban and rural residents is slower than that of GDP, where the income growth rate of rural residents

TABLE 4
China's GDP Growth and Its Components 2005–10 (Per Cent of GDP)

GDP growth and its components/year	2005	2006	2007	2008	2009	2010
Real GDP growth rate	11.3	12.7	14.2	9.6	9.1	10.3
Urban disposal income growth	9.6	10.4	12.2	8.4	9.8	7.8
Rural net income growth	6.2	7.4	9.5	8.0	8.5	10.9
Labour's share in GDP	47.7	47.1	46.6	N.A.	N.A.	N.A.
Contribution of consumption	37.9	40.0	39.2	43.5	45.4	48.0^E
Contribution of investment	39.0	43.9	42.7	47.5	95.2	65.9^E
Contribution of net exports	23.1	16.1	18.1	9.0	−40.6	−14.0^E
Savings to expenditure approach of GDP	47.1	49.3	50.5	51.6	52.0	52.0^E
Investment to expenditure approach of GDP	41.6	41.8	41.7	43.9	47.7	49.6^E
Savings–investment gap	5.5	7.5	8.8	7.7	4.4	2.4^E

Source: Data from 2005 to 2009 are from corresponding years of *China Statistical Yearbook*; Data of 2010 are drawn from 2010 *Statistical Communiqué on the National Economic and Social Development*. Because of data limitation, we use monthly growth rate data of total retail sales of consumer goods, urban fixed asset investment and net export to estimate the contribution of consumption, investment and net export and the savings and investment shares of expenditure approach of GDP (denoted with superscript E). It shall also be noted that data of labour's share of income approach of GDP from 2008 to 2010 are not available.

is the lowest. The discordant pace between economic development and income growth will naturally lead to labour's share decreasing. Labour's share has decreased from 51.4 per cent to 46.6 per cent between 1995 and 2007.[9] The phenomenon of capital's share of increasing has attracted attention academically and publically. We argue that the investment led economic development mode is one of the key reasons for this. We can find from Table 3 that investment's contribution to economic growth is always higher during 2005–10, where its contribution reached its highest level of 95.2 per cent because of the stimulus package. The result of investment-led economic growth is that the rising status of capital and natural resources (especially land) relative to oversupply of labour in competitive markets. This pattern will lead to the rise of income share of capitalists (entrepreneurs) and landlords (local government), and the fall of income share of labourers.

c. Explanation of International and Domestic Imbalance

The connection between dual imbalance has not received enough attention. Domestic GDP accounts detail the phenomenon of the savings investment gap,[10] while the international balance sheets show us a large current account surplus. The relationships between international and domestic imbalance can be illustrated by

---

[9] These data are a rough calculation of raw data of income approach of GDP, and the refined measurement of labor's share can be obtained by dealing with income tax and proprietary income (Zhou et al., 2010).

[10] We can see from the last row of Table 4 that the savings–investment gap has reached 8.8 per cent of GDP in 2007.

the linkage between investment, export and consumption. On one side, investment led economic growth will create excess production capacity. On the other side, it will cause low cost competition among labour, causing the lag of income growth compared with economic development and the decrease of labour's share in national income.

The sharp drop in labour's share in national income will further cause the decline in the ratio of consumption to GDP. Therefore, the domestic imbalance mainly reflects the contradiction between high investment and low consumption. This pattern will be reinforced to the extent that the economy deviates from the balanced growth path and risks economic downturn. The strategy for tackling this contradiction is either to shut down enterprises and tolerate economic recession or to export. Lucky for China, it perfectly embraces the waves of economic globalisation by reform and opening up. It uses cheap labour as its comparative advantage to export and gains competitiveness by producing manufacturing goods for the world. Therefore, investment and exports become the two main engines for pulling China's economy.

However, the choice to transfer domestic imbalance to international imbalance is not stable. The sharp contraction of external demand caused by the financial crisis suddenly shut down the export engine for economic growth. In turn, international imbalance has been alleviated, while domestic imbalance has been intensified. The momentum of investment led growth unconsciously forces the Chinese government to use stimulus policies, relying heavily on investment to save the economy in the face of economic crisis. Although this policy has effectively prevented economic recession, the domestic imbalance, to some extent, is worsened.

4. THE LOGIC BEHIND CHINA'S POLICYMAKING

Luo and Zhang (2010) adopt a political economy approach to comment on trade policies for the 2008 TPR. They summarise three major features for China's trade policy by comparing China with other developed countries (e.g. United States). They argue that the features of China's trade policy are 'top down', 'outside in' and 'pro-government' versus 'bottom up', 'inside out' and 'pro-market' in the United States. We agree and appreciate their insights.

Unlike them, this paper will emphasise more the logic behind the policymaking procedure from a different perspective. And we mainly focus on macro-level policy, taking trade policy as an organic component.

a. Priority of Three Major Objectives for PolicyMaking

To understand the internal logic of policymaking, we should first clarify the priority of major objectives. We argue that there are three major objectives with different levels of priority. First, promoting economic growth is the fundamental requirement. Second, maintaining social stability.[11] Third, if the aforementioned two objectives are fulfilled, the internal requirement of the market system such as protecting property rights and building fair competition rules will be considered afterwards.

Many examples can be illustrated for testing the priorities of three major objectives. In a decentralised government structure, local governments always put 'economic growth' as their top priority. Competition among local government in attracting FDI is a perfect example for illustrating the importance of the growth objective.

Short-term stability is taken into consideration despite the fact that polices will have a favourable effect on long-term growth. For example, the 1987–88 price reform has fuelled rapid inflation and panic purchasing which forced the central government to cease the reform plan. Deng Xiaoping said afterwards, 'rapid growth is a good thing, however, too fast growth will also bring troubles . . . we have too much courage, what we need now is stability. Our task now is to keep the stability for a big country with 1 billion people'.[12] This is a good example for illustrating the importance of stability for the short-run.

After the fulfilment of economic growth and stability, the internal requirement of market system is taken into consideration. Economic policy over the last 30 years always puts fairness in second place. However, the effective operation of the market economy requires predictive and transparent rules. Recent studies show that urban–rural income inequality and income inequality between urban industries has increased rather than decreased during the marketisation process. It implies that China's transition does not evolve to a competitive market economy system which proves the lowest status of fairness objective (Chen et al., 2010).

b. Policymaking Compatible with Priority of Objectives

In fact, policymaking is always compatible with the priority of three major objectives. During the recent decade, the Chinese government becomes more concerned about balanced structure and more equal distribution. These changes of policies are always considered as a change of priority of objectives by foreign observers. They conclude that the current policies emphasise more fairness rather than growth. Unlike them, we argue that the priority of objectives remains unchanged because government has realised that increasing income inequality would hinder further growth of the economy. In other words, when economic inequality poses threats to the 'growth' objective, the government then will have

---

[11] The social stability includes economic and political stability.
[12] The more complete speech can be found in CCCPC Party Literature Research Office (2004).

the impetus to improve distribution. Therefore, the priority of three major objectives for Chinese government is clear and consistent over time.

However, the real difficulty for the government is to cope with short-run and long-run economic growth, which is also mentioned by Luo and Zhang (2010). On the one hand, government tries to adjust its economic structure and the development mode to maintain long-run economic growth. On the other hand, the structural reform may have negative impacts on the short-run growth rate. The global financial crisis increases the possibility and extent of such negative impacts and puts government in an awkward position in choosing between long-run and short-run growth. As a result, government finally chooses a strong stimulus package to maintain short-run growth. The reason is quite straightforward. The external shock became more urgent than economic imbalance. Therefore, the government will choose policies that tackle the most urgent issues and have the lowest side effects.

This logic can be easily applied to the evolution of trade policy. Before the crisis, the government tried to improve the trade structure by tightening policy on processing trade and emphasising an increasing sophistication of trade products. However, drastic changes in policies have been made when the financial crisis hit China. Thus, loosening export tax rebates and promoting processing trade became major polices in face of global financial crisis.

c. Reasons of Pattern of China's Policymaking Procedure

The aforementioned statement shows that the policy-making procedure can be summarised as a trinity of economic growth, social stability and market reform. On one side, policymakers always take the market reform as a means for complying with the other two objectives so that the market reform must take the economic growth as its objective, and social stability as its constraint. On the other side, the institutional transition from a planned economy to a market one is a systematic transformation process which cannot be accomplished by a single action. Therefore, the market reform of China is a gradual process, and the market economy system featured with fair competition and effective operation has not been completely built. Unlike other transitional economies which seek to build an 'idealized' and given market economy model,[13] the major objective for market reform in China is growth and stability, which is the secret for China to keep both high growth and social stability at the same time. However, the gradual reform strategy also results

---

[13] For example, the market reform of East Germany took the system of West Germany as its main objectives. Naturally, Former Soviet Union countries took the market system of Europe or the United States as their major objectives.

in a very long transitional process so that the 'idealised' market economy system which is accepted by western standards has not been taken into form.

We shall also bear in mind that history is also important in understanding China's policymaking. China not only has differences of degree of economic development between urban and rural areas and among different geographic regions, but also has differences of civil rights because of institutional segmentation and ownership discrimination.[14] These differences of civil rights cannot be eliminated overnight so that the gradual reform and transition may be the only feasible and right choice from an historical point of view. It is no wonder that the requirement of equality and justice cannot be fulfilled easily.

5. STRUCTURAL REFORM FOR THE POST-CRISIS ERA

As mentioned earlier, the current unbalanced economic development mode cannot be sustained and will change in the future. This is not only a consensus of economists at home and abroad, but also a striving goal for the Chinese government. However, the change of the pattern of international and domestic unbalance is not an easy road, and China will face great and formidable challenges by changing its economic development mode.

a. The Consensus of Changing the Economic Development Mode

Like many foreign scholars, economists at home have also realised issues constraining the future development the of China's economy (Yao, 2007b; Lu and Luo, 2010). The decomposition of economic growth of China shows that the main contribution to economic growth is capital, while the contributions of the total factor productivity (TFP) and labour have been relatively small since reform and opening up (Wang, 2000; Gapinski, 2001; Chow and Lin, 2002; Wang and Yao, 2003; Lin and Ren, 2006; Lin and Su, 2007).[15] In terms of these imbalance issues, the consensus shared among economists is that past extensive and capital-driven economic growth will be transformed into technology- and talent-driven economic development. In other words, we should be more concerned about long-run, high efficiency, inclusive and sustainable growth and emphasise equal income distribution and social justice so as to change the impetus structure of economic growth and jointly improve the internal and external economic imbalance.

---

[14] For a fuller discussion about the evolvement of differences of civil rights in China, see Yao's (2007b) paper on topics of evolution of labor market in China.
[15] All these studies indicate that TFP contribution is no more than 28 per cent, while the contribution of the capital is bigger than 50 per cent.

b. Objectives and Measures for Changing the Economic Development Mode

The change of policies can be best illustrated in the '12th Five-Year Plan of National Economy and Social Development PRC', which was released in March 2011. In the '12th Five-Year Plan', the Chinese government has put the change of economic development mode as the main focus of policy, and it aims to change economic development from investment driven to consumption driven, from physical capital driven to human capital driven so the economy will be geared more towards the domestic consumer and less dependent on exports. The plan also emphasises that the policies will mainly improve and ensure people's livelihood as the essential starting point and final destination. Therefore, the government will improve income distribution by promoting income growth higher than GDP growth.

The reform of trade policy is consistent with the change of economic development mode. China will devote itself to promoting global trade liberalisation and balancing international and domestic economic accounts. In the '12th Five-Year Plan', the government clearly states that future foreign trade development will transfer from scale expansion to quality and benefit promotion, from cost advantage to comprehensive competitive advantage. It will mainly use three measures to implement this transition. First, it will cultivate new advantages with core competitiveness on technology, brand, quality and service. Second, it will actively increase the import of products of advanced technology, key components and parts, domestic scare resources, energy conservation and environment protection. It will take imports as an important mediator in realising macroeconomic balance and achieving structural adjustment. Third, it will promote the export of services, enhance the openness of the services sector and increase the share of services trade in the total trade.

c. A Tough Task for Changing the Economic Development Mode

There is a good omen in achieving structural change. The international accounts show that the share of current account surplus in GDP in 2010 has reached the lowest point 5.3 per cent for the recent five years, and the share of trade surplus in GDP even reaches 4.3 per cent. In February 2011, the trade deficit of US$7.3 billion occurred for the first time. The domestic accounts also show that the savings to investment gap has reached its historical lowest point 2.4 per cent. These newest macro data indicate that the imbalanced feature of international and domestic accounts has alleviated, and the economic development is going to achieve an equilibrium state.

However, there are great difficulties during the transition process despite of the effort and devotion that Chinese government has already made. A very good example is that the emphasis on changing the economic growth mode and committing scientific development has already been brought forward in the '11th Five-Year Plan'. However, the global economic crisis postpones China's pace of structural reform to maintain the economic growth and employment as the priorities. Meanwhile, the momentum of the old system is still large and the current adjustment faces grate challenges. Because of the regional disparities of economic development of China, inland areas still pursue the investment-driven growth strategies as their main policies. In 2009, the investment rate of central and western area of China reached 57.6 per cent and 64.3 per cent, respectively, which are higher than eastern area by 9 and 16 per cent. Third, as a developing country, China undertakes three major transition tasks, that is, industrialisation, urbanisation and marketisation. Therefore, the change of the economic development will become more complex by coordinating diversified objectives. For the aforesaid reasons, we believe that the successful change of the unbalanced pattern and past economic development mode will not only requires China's own endeavour, but also require a loose external environment.

REFERENCES

Bertola, G. and A. Ichino (1995), 'Wage Inequality and Unemployment: United States vs. Europe', *NBER Macroeconomics Annual*, **10**, 1, 13–54.
Branstetter, L. and N. Lardy (2008), 'China's Embrace of Globalization', in L. Brandt and T. G. Rawski (eds.), *China's Great Economic Transformation* (New York: Cambridge University Press), 633–82.
CCCPC Party Literature Research Office (2004), *A Chronicle of Deng Xiao Ping: 1975–1997* (Beijing: Central Party Literature Press).
Chen, Z., G.-H. Wan and M. Lu (2011), 'Inter-industry Income Inequality: An Increasingly Important Cause of Income Disparity in Urban China-A Regression-based Decomposition', *Social Sciences in China*, **3**, 1, 65–76.
Chow, G. C. and A.-L. Lin (2002), 'Accounting for Economic Growth in Taiwan and Mainland China: A Comparative Analysis', *Journal of Comparative Economics*, **30**, 3, 507–30.
Freeman, R. B. (1995), 'Are Your Wages Set in Beijing', *Journal of Economic Perspectives*, **9**, 3, 15–32.
Gapinski, J. H. (2001), 'The Panda That Grew', *China Economic Review*, **12**, 4, 263–79.
Guha, K. (2009), 'Paulson Says Crisis Sown by Imbalance', *Financial Times*, 1 January.
Lin, J. Y. and R.-E. Ren (2006), 'East Asian Miracle Debate Revisited', *Economic Research Journal*, **6**, 1, 4–12.
Lin, J. Y. and J. Su (2007), 'On the Change of China's Economic Growth Mode', *Management World*, **11**, 1, 5–13.
Lu, X.-X. and X.-F. Luo (2011), 'Three Major Issues of Government Constraining the Change of Economic Development Mode in China', *Finance and Trade Economics*, **11**, 1, 112–7.
Luo, C.-Y. and J. Zhang (2010), 'China Trade Policy Review: A Political Economy Approach', *The World Economy*, **33**, 11,1390–413.
National Bureau of Statistics (2010), *China Statistical Yearbook* (Beijing: China Statistics Press).
PRC China (2011), 'The 12th Five-Year Plan of National Economic and Social Development People's Republic of China', Xinhua News Agency, 16 March.
Sachs, J. D. and H. J. Shatz (1996), 'U.S. Trade with Developing Countries and Wage Inequality', *American Economic Review*, **86**, 2, 234–39.

Song, Z., K. Storesletten and F. Zilibott (2011), 'Growing Like China', *American Economic Review*, **101**, 1, 202–41.

Stiglitz, J. (2011), 'We Face A Marked Global Reversal', *Financial Times*, 7 January.

Wang, X.-L. (2000), 'Sustainability of China's Economic Growth and Institutional Changes', *Economic Research Journal*, **7**, 1, 3–15.

Wang, Y. and Y.-D. Yao (2003), 'Sources of China's Economic Growth 1952–1999: Incorporating Human Capital Accumulation', *China Economic Review*, **14**, 1, 32–52.

World Trade Organization (2006), 'China Trade Policy Review 2006', WT/TPR/S/161, WT/TPR/G161, WT/TPR/M/161. Available at http://www.wto.org/english/tratop_e/tpr_e/tp262_e.htm (accessed 18 October 2011).

World Trade Organization (2008), 'China Trade Policy Review 2008', WT/TPR/S/199, WT/TPR/G/199 WT/TPR/M/199. Available at http://www.wto.org/english/tratop_e/tpr_e/tp299_e.htm (accessed 18 October 2011).

World Trade Organization (2010), 'China Trade Policy Review 2010', WT/TPR/S/230, WT/TPR/G/230, WT/TPR/M/230. Available at http://www.wto.org/english/tratop_e/tpr_e/tp330_e.htm (accessed 18 October 2011).

Yao, X.-G. (2007a), 'Reforming China and Its Gradually Changing Labor Market', Working Paper Presented in the 68th Conferences of American Society for Public Administration (ASPA), USA.

Yao, X.-G. (2007b), 'Dual Constraints and Macroeconomic Control', *Economic Issues in China*, **2**, 1, 22–30.

Zhou, M.-H., W. Xiao and X.-G. Yao (2010), 'Unbalanced Economic Growth and Uneven National Income Distribution: Evidence from China', Working Paper Series of Institute for Research on Labor and Employment of University of California, Los Angles, CA.

3

Free Trade in Agriculture and Global Poverty

Maurizio Bussolo, Rafael De Hoyos and Denis Medvedev

1. INTRODUCTION

𝔍N most cases, trade liberalisation is welfare increasing, but it also brings about large income redistribution. While the empirical literature generally finds the aggregate gains to be small – on the order of a few percentage points of initial GDP – 'the [static] efficiency consequences of trade reform pale in comparison with its redistributive effects' (Rodrik, 1998). These effects often create complicated policy challenges both at the domestic and at the international levels because, in most cases, losers tend to be a smaller and more vocal group than winners.[1] The recent collapse of the Doha Round is an example of such tensions, with disputes over the reduction of agricultural distortions stalling the progress of the entire negotiations.

The authors are grateful to Kym Anderson, Hans Timmer, Ernesto Valenzuela, Dominique van der Mensbrugghe, participants of the 2007 'Agricultural Price Distortions, Inequality and Poverty' conference at the World Bank, 2007 LACEA conference at the Universidad de los Andes, and 2008 GTAP conference in Helsinki for helpful comments and suggestions. All remaining errors are ours. The findings, interpretations and conclusions expressed in this paper are entirely those of the authors. They do not necessarily reflect the view of the World Bank, its executive directors, or the countries they represent.

[1] According to Anderson and Martin (2005), self-interested vocal groups lobbying hard for excluding agricultural liberalisation from multilateral negotiations include 'not just farmers in the highly protecting countries and net food importing developing countries but also those food exporters receiving preferential access to those markets including holders of tariff rate quotas, members of regional trading agreements and parties to non-reciprocal preference agreements including all least-developed countries'.

Resolving the current impasse could not only imply a solution to the distributional tension between countries – reconciling the demands of developing and agriculture exporting countries on one side and (mainly) high-income countries with large domestic support on the other – but also narrow income disparities *within* countries by reducing or eliminating the urban bias in the protection structure of many developing nations.[2] This paper, using an *ex-ante* simulation analysis, assesses the likelihood of these developments by addressing the following three questions: (i) What is the likely reduction in global inequality if all agriculture trade distortions are removed? (ii) To what extent can this reduction be attributed to inequality changes between countries and within countries? (iii) What happens to global poverty and to poverty incidence in specific countries? A major result of this paper is that while the global impacts are generally mild, the likely changes at the country and regional level are much more pronounced, therefore highlighting the need for global coordination.

The paper is organised as follows. The next section presents the data used in the analysis and establishes some basic facts about the structure of global poverty and global income distribution. Section 3 discusses the methodology behind the analysis, and Section 4 presents the results. Section 5 concludes with some final remarks.

2. WHAT IS AT STAKE? THE INITIAL POSITION OF FARMERS AND THE POTENTIAL BENEFITS OR COST OF AGRICULTURAL DISTORTIONS

Almost 45 per cent of the population in the world lives in households where agricultural activities represent the main occupation of the head. And a large share of this agriculture-dependent group, close to 32 per cent, is poor. Agriculture households contribute disproportionably to global poverty: three out of every four poor people belong to this group (see Table 1). So changing economic opportunities in agriculture can significantly affect global poverty and inequality. The specific opportunity considered in detail here is the removal of agricultural trade barriers. Direct effects of this liberalisation will be changes in the international prices of agricultural products and in the returns of factors used intensively in agriculture with these changes determining winners and losers. Before considering these effects in detail, this section describes what is at stake by considering the socioeconomic characteristics of the agricultural population.

---

[2] Krueger et al. (1991) is perhaps the most well-known study documenting this anti-agriculture bias in developing counties. For 18 countries included in the study, policy interventions induced a 30 per cent decline in a price index of agricultural products relative to a non-agricultural price index. In fact, a key motivation for the current study is to revisit these former estimates and assess where the anti-agriculture bias stands now.

TABLE 1

Poverty is Higher among Agricultural Households even if Their Incomes are Less Unequal

	Gini (%)	Pop Shares (%)	Average Monthly Income (2000, US Purchasing Power Parity)	1-dollar Poverty Incidence (%)	Poverty Share (%)
Agriculture	44.9	44.8	65.4	31.7	75.9
Non-agriculture	62.8	55.2	328.9	8.1	24.0
World	67.0	100	210.8	18.7	100

Source: Global Income Distribution Dynamics database (http://www.world-bank.org/prospects/gidd).

This initial descriptive analysis is based on the Global Income Distribution Dynamics (GIDD) data set that has been recently developed at the World Bank.[3] The GIDD data set consists of 73 detailed household surveys for low- and middle-income countries, complemented with more aggregate information on income distribution for 25 high-income and 22 developing countries.[4] Together, data on these 120 countries cover more than 90 per cent of the global population. Country coverage varies by region: while the GIDD data set includes more than 97 per cent of population in East Asia and Pacific, Eastern Europe and Central Asia, Latin America, and South Asia, coverage in sub-Saharan Africa and Middle East and North Africa is limited to 76 and 58 per cent of population, respectively. Among the detailed surveys, the majority (54) use per capita consumption as the welfare indicator, while the remaining surveys – all but one for countries in Latin America – include only per capita income as a measure of household welfare. Both income and consumption data are monthly; the data are standardised to the year 2000 and are expressed in 1993 purchasing power parity (PPP) prices for consistency with the 1- and 2-dollar-a-day poverty lines, which are calculated at 1993 PPP exchange rates.[5]

---

[3] The description of the data set may be found at the following website: http://www.world-bank.org/prospects/gidd

[4] This more aggregate information usually consists of 20 data points for each country, with each data point representing the average per capita income (or consumption) of 5 per cent of the country's population. In the absence of full survey data, using these 'vintile' data provides a close approximation to most economy-wide measures of inequality.

[5] The adjustment procedure for expressing welfare indicators in 1993 international dollars (PPP) is as follows. First, for countries with a survey year different than 2000, the welfare indicator (household per capita income or consumption) is scaled to the year 2000 using the cumulative growth in real income per capita between the survey year and 2000. Then, the welfare indicator is converted to 1993 national prices by multiplying the welfare indicator by the ratio of consumer price index (CPI) in 1993 to the CPI in the survey year. Finally, the welfare indicator is converted to 1993 international prices by multiplying the outcome of the previous calculations by the 1993 PPP exchange rate.

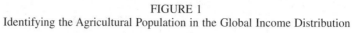

FIGURE 1

Identifying the Agricultural Population in the Global Income Distribution

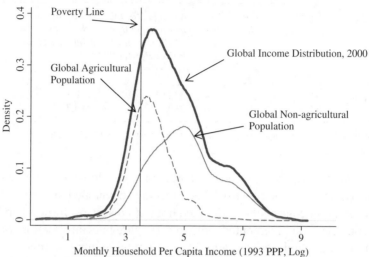

Three facts about the agricultural sector determine the overall welfare effects of a global-scale removal of agricultural distortions: (i) the proportion of the world population whose real incomes depend on the agricultural sector; (ii) the initial position of the agricultural population in the global income distribution; and (iii) the dispersion of incomes among the agricultural population.[6] Using the GIDD data set, Figure 1 shows a kernel density for the global income distribution of household per capita income/consumption and kernel *densities* for incomes/consumption of the population in and out of the agricultural sector, respectively.[7] The area below the kernel *density* for the agricultural sector is equal to 0.45, showing that 45 per cent of the world population relies on agriculture for its livelihood. The distribution of the agricultural population is located to the left of the non-agricultural distribution implying that households in the agricultural sector earn, on average, lower incomes than their counterparts in other sectors. In PPP US dollars, the average agricultural household's per capita monthly income is 65

---

[6] The estimates of the welfare effects of a global agricultural liberalisation will also depend on the pattern of initial distortions (tariffs and subsidies) and, at least in the short term where no adjustment is possible, on the number of net consumers and net producers. Notice that, as explained in Section 3, our methodology allows for adjustments in the patterns of production (employment by sector changes) and consumption and thus consider the longer term.

[7] The distributions for the agricultural and non-agricultural populations are not, strictly speaking, density functions since the area below the curve do not add to 1. The densities of the agricultural and non-agricultural population had been rescaled so that the area under the curve represents the proportion of the world population within these two groups.

TABLE 2
Characteristics of the Poor (for Developing Countries Only)

Sector of Employment	Primary School Completed (%)	Age	Household Size	Female Headed (%)
Agricultural	32.29	44.7	7.0	8.7
Non-agricultural	45.43	44.5	7.0	14

Notes:
(1) Primary school completed and age refers to the household head.
(2) Using data from the Global Income Distribution Dynamics.

dollars, just 20 per cent of the 329 dollars of per capita income earned by the average households in the non-agriculture group, see Table 1. The differences in shape between the two distributions corroborates what Kuznets hypothesised more than 50 years ago, i.e. incomes in the traditional sector are less dispersed than in the modern industries. A more egalitarian traditional sector is depicted in the form of a taller and thinner distribution for agricultural population in Figure 1.

Income inequality can be estimated from the global income distribution data depicted in Figure 1. The Gini index for the world is equal to 67 per cent, which denotes a high level of inequality. In fact, the global Gini is about 28 points worse than that of the United States and even higher than the level observed in extremely unequal countries such as Mexico. As Bourguignon et al. (2004) noted 'if the world were a country, it would be among the most unequal countries of the world'. How much of this inequality can be explained by the disparity on average incomes between the agricultural group and the rest? Inequality decomposition analysis shows that a quarter of global income disparities can be explained by the difference in average incomes between the two groups of households and the remaining three-quarters are due to within group income variation.

Based on the pre-established poverty line of 1 dollar (PPP) per day, the GIDD global income data also provide information about the differences in poverty incidence among the two population subgroups. Despite the fact that incomes are better distributed among the agricultural population (the Gini coefficient is 18 points lower in agriculture), lower average incomes in this sector result in higher poverty incidence: 31.7 per cent of agricultural households are poor versus 8.1 per cent among the non-agricultural households.

In terms of personal characteristics of the poor in and out of the agricultural sector, Table 2 shows that no noticeable differences are observed on the average age of the head and household size. However, poor people in agriculture tend to have lower education levels: just below a third of them has completed primary education. In agriculture, poor households headed by a woman are a small minority, close to 8 per cent, significantly below the 14 per cent observed in the non-agriculture segment (see Table 2).

FIGURE 2

Income Levels and Employment in Agriculture: A Negative Cross-Section Relationship

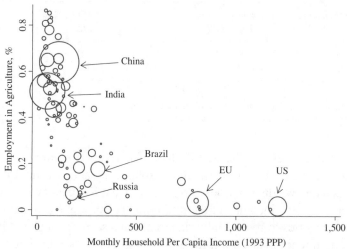

Up to this point, the welfare information on agricultural and non-agricultural populations has been derived by agglomerating all households within these two groups irrespectively of their nationality. In fact, the kernel *densities* in Figure 1 exploit full income heterogeneity across households including variations between and within countries. Countries display large differences in terms of their population size, their level of development and the importance of the agricultural sector in their economies. These three country-specific characteristics are important determinants of the change of global poverty and global inequality. Clearly, as shown by Figure 2, global poverty would be strongly reduced in cases where China and India move towards higher income levels. Given their initial large share of global population and their position in the global income distribution, the economic expansion of these two giants is a key factor shaping the evolution of the world economy.[8] Figure 2 also depicts a negative relationship between income levels and share of workers in agriculture, and although this relationship is imperfectly inferred from a cross-section of countries at a particular point in time, it still suggests that profound structural shifts will likely affect income distribution within countries. Clearly, the development challenges of a transition from an agriculture-based economy towards a more industrialised one, or even the management of the shocks originating from (agriculture) trade policy reform differ enormously across countries. Given the large variation in the proportion of the

[8] For a specific analysis of the importance of China and India for global growth and income distribution, see Bussolo et al. (2007).

FIGURE 3
Inequality Variation Across Countries and Sectors

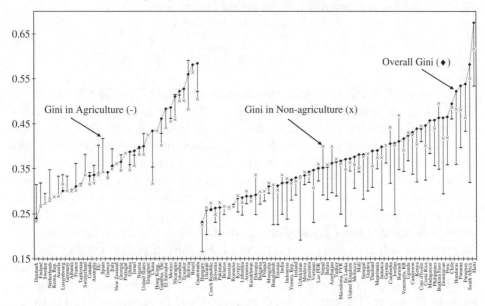

Note:
Authors calculations based on Global Income Distribution Dynamics data set using developing countries information only.

population whose incomes depend on the agricultural sector, the income effects following a removal of agricultural distortions would be highly different *between countries*.

An important element hidden in Figure 1 is the degree of cross-country variation in income inequality. Figure 3 shows that the difference in the Gini coefficient between countries is enormous, with former communist countries like Romania and Hungary showing an index below 0.3, whereas in highly unequal countries such as South Africa and Mozambique, the index reaches values above 0.6. Once again, the tendency of higher inequality within the non-agriculture group observed at the global level is corroborated by the analysis of country-specific inequality. For more than three-quarters of the countries included in our data (56 of 73), Gini indicators of inequality within the non-agricultural group are higher than those of the agricultural group (Figure 3).

A global trade reform removing agricultural distortions is expected to reallocate resources between agricultural and non-agricultural sectors at the international level and within national states. Given global variations in: (i) the importance of the agricultural sector; (ii) the agriculture to non-agriculture income premium; and (ii) the within-sector income inequality, the resource reallocation following trade reform will have significant distributional effects *between and within countries.* Can economic theory provide some guidance on the expected global welfare effects following the removal of agricultural distortions?

3. METHODOLOGY

According to Winters (2000), Hoekman et al. (2002) and McCulloch et al. (2002), trade liberalisation and household welfare are linked via prices, factor markets and consumer preferences. International prices of agricultural products will, most likely, increase as a result of the removal of agricultural trade barriers such as subsidies and tariffs (Anderson, 2003). Assuming some degree of pass-through, the increase in international prices will be followed by a rise in domestic agricultural prices enhancing a redistribution of resources from non-agricultural to the agricultural sector of the economy. Based on Figure 1, such redistribution could help reduce global poverty and inequality. However, household consumption patterns will also change as a result of the shift in prices, making the link between agricultural trade liberalisation and global household welfare a complex one. Finally, factor prices will also change after trade liberalisation, changing real incomes of households that are not directly involved in agricultural production.

The transition from trade theory to real-world analysis presents serious challenges. A sound empirical strategy has to estimate the effects of the reform on: prices, monetary incomes (via profits in the case of farm households and returns to factors of production for non-farm households), consumption and transfers.[9] The framework used in this paper, and described in more details below, accounts for the impact of agricultural trade liberalisation through changes in consumer welfare because of changes in prices of final products, changes in household incomes as a result of changes in returns to factors of production and sectoral allocation of labour in agricultural and non-agricultural sectors.

The empirical analysis in this paper relies on the GIDD data and methodology.[10] The GIDD, developed at the Development Economic Prospects Group of the World Bank, combines a consistent set of price and volume changes from a global computable general equilibrium (CGE) model with microdata at the household level to create a simulated or counterfactual income distribution capturing the welfare effects of the policy under evaluation.[11] Therefore, the GIDD has the

---

[9] For an empirical application of trade's effect on Mexican household welfare taking into account these effects, see Nicita (2004).
[10] A detailed methodological description of the GIDD can be found in Bussolo et al. (2010), as well as in the GIDD website referenced earlier.
[11] The GIDD uses the LINKAGE model as the global CGE framework; see van der Mensbrugghe (2005) for a detailed description of LINKAGE.

FIGURE 4
Global Income Distribution Dynamics Methodological Framework

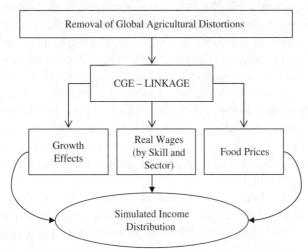

ability to map CGE-consistent macroeconomic outcomes to disaggregated household survey data.

The GIDD's framework is based on microsimulation methodologies developed in the recent literature, including Bourguignon and Pereira da Silva (2003); Chen and Ravallion (2003); Ferreira and Leite (2003, 2004); and Bussolo et al. (2005). The starting point is the global income distribution in 2000, assembled using data from household surveys.[12] The 'simulated' distribution is then obtained by applying three main exogenous changes to the initial distribution: (i) shifts in the sectoral composition of employment; (ii) economic growth, including changes in relative wages across skills and sectors; and (iii) changes in real income derived from the shifts in food prices.

The empirical framework is depicted in Figure 4. The starting point is the price and quantity effects following the removal of agricultural distortions, which are computed using the global CGE model (top part of Figure 4). The CGE will compute the values of the three variables linking the macro- and microlevels of the model (middle part of Figure 4): overall economic growth, real wage premiums among agricultural/non-agricultural and skilled/unskilled groups, and the consumption (or real income) effects brought about by the change in relative price of food. These CGE results are passed-on to the household survey data, creating a new, simulated household income distribution (bottom link in Figure 4). Distribution and poverty comparisons between the initial and the counterfactual

---

[12] Throughout the paper, when we talk about the global distribution, we are indeed referring to the GIDD's sample covering 92 per cent of the world population.

income distributions will capture the welfare effects of the removal of global agricultural distortions. By taking into account labour market (returns to skills in and out the agricultural sector) and consumption effects while evaluating macropolicies, GIDD's framework closely maps the theoretical linkages outlined above.[13]

In the real world, the changes depicted in Figure 4 take place simultaneously, but in the GIDD's simplified framework, they are accommodated in a sequential fashion. In the first step, consistent with an overall growth rate of real income per capita, changes in labour remuneration by skill level and sectoral location are applied to each worker in the sample depending on their education and sector of employment. In the second step, real household incomes are affected by the change in the price of food versus non-food; households with a higher share of household income allocated to food consumption will bear the larger impact after a change in the price of food.

The sequential changes described earlier reshape national income distribution under a set of strong assumptions. In particular, income inequality within population subgroups formed by skills and sector of employment is assumed to remain constant after the trade reform. Moreover, data limitations affect estimates of the initial inequality and its evolution. Although consumption expenditure is a more reliable welfare measure than income, and its distribution is normally more equal than the distribution of income, consumption data are not available for all countries' surveys. To get a global picture, this study had to include: countries for which only income data were available and countries with consumption information. Finally, measurement errors implicit in purchasing power parity exchange rates, which have been used to convert local currency units, also affect comparability across countries. The resulting simulated income distribution should thus not be seen as a *forecast* of what the future distribution might look like; instead, it should be interpreted as the result of an exercise that captures the *ceteris paribus* distributional effect of agricultural trade liberalisation.

4. WHAT HAPPENS TO POVERTY AND INCOME DISTRIBUTION WHEN AGRICULTURE TRADE DISTORTIONS ARE REMOVED?

In this section, we link the macro-outcomes of global agricultural trade reform to the changes in the distribution of income *between* and *within* countries. Our analysis is carried out in three stages. First, we briefly examine the macroeconomic results of the LINKAGE model, focusing on the variables that are used to change the household survey data. Second, we consider the income distribution results

---

[13] The GIDD does not take into account the welfare impacts via changes in transfers resulting from the trade reform.

from a global perspective, quantifying the likely changes in global poverty and inequality and identifying groups of countries and individuals that are likely to benefit the most (least) from agricultural trade reform. Thirdly, we assess the potential trends in the distribution of income within countries, identifying countries where inequality pressures may heighten and thus erode support for additional reforms.

a. Macroeconomic General Equilibrium Results

The LINKAGE simulation analysis has been carried out with the 7.0 prerelease of the GTAP database, which disaggregates global trade into bilateral flows between 101 countries/regions in 57 commodity groups. The base year for the simulations is 2004, and the data take into account changes in the global trade and tariff structure owing to the implementation of the Uruguay Round commitments, the EU enlargement, China's accession to the WTO and implementation of most major preferential trade agreements. The model is solved in a comparative static mode, which means that simulations are implemented as one-time shocks and do not take into account potential growth effects through changes in capital accumulation rates or variations in productivity.

Our main simulation envisions the full removal of import tariffs and export taxes/subsidies on agriculture and food products around the globe. The liberalisation schedule includes 17 of 57 commodities in GTAP, and the initial level of protection by exporter is shown in Table 3.[14,15]

Because of the removal of barriers to trade in agriculture and food products, global consumption rises by 0.29 per cent, two-thirds of the improvement expected under a full trade liberalisation scenario where tariff for all good are eliminated. Low- and middle-income countries gain more than the average, with consumption rising by 0.47 per cent in the developing world compared to 0.24 per cent for high-income countries. Following the removal of agricultural distortions, 50 of 60 LINKAGE country/regions – representing nearly 95 per cent of the world – experience positive changes in consumption (Figure 5).

There are three main channels that transmit the trade reform shocks to household consumption in the LINKAGE model and help explain the heterogeneity of the results in Figure 5. The first channel is the changes in the terms of trade, the ratio of export prices to import prices without taking into account domestic price distortions (i.e. own import tariffs and export taxes/subsidies). Net exporters of agriculture and food, such as Brazil, Ecuador and New Zealand, reap significant welfare gains when the world export prices of these commodities rise by 8, 19

---

[14] Trade in other beverages and tobacco is excluded from the liberalisation list.
[15] An alternative scenario where all border distortions are removed is considered in the working paper version (see Bussolo et al., 2009).

TABLE 3
Developing Countries Face Higher Tariffs than High-Income Countries

Importer	Low- and Middle-income Countries		High-income Countries	
	Tariffs Faced (%)	Exports (% of Total)	Tariffs Faced (%)	Exports (% of Total)
Exporter				
World total	13.0	31.5	10.6	68.5
High-income countries	12.9	23.7	7.8	76.3
United States	10.0	48.3	24.1	51.7
EU 15	14.7	15.0	2.9	85.0
Low- and middle-income countries	13.0	44.3	16.6	55.7
East Asia and Pacific	16.5	41.4	23.7	58.6
China	16.7	25.3	27.6	74.7
Indonesia	15.6	57.6	11.3	42.4
Europe and Central Asia	9.2	51.7	9.3	48.3
Poland	12.3	35.0	3.6	65.0
Russia	13.3	59.0	21.4	41.0
Latin America and the Caribbean	14.1	40.9	16.5	59.1
Brazil	18.2	47.9	24.3	52.1
Mexico	16.2	7.4	5.4	92.6
Middle East and North Africa	10.4	55.1	12.2	44.9
Egypt	9.4	55.3	12.8	44.7
Morocco	12.8	17.7	7.8	82.3
South Asia	12.0	57.2	15.4	42.8
India	12.3	55.5	15.5	44.5
Pakistan	9.5	72.8	27.4	27.2
Sub-Saharan Africa	9.7	39.1	9.8	60.9
South Africa	13.5	39.4	8.8	60.6
Nigeria	10.9	17.6	1.6	82.4

Source: Authors' calculations with GTAP7.0 database.

Notes:
'Tariffs faced' column shows the import-weighted average tariff imposed by the column country/region on exports from the row country/region. 'Exports' column shows the exports of the row country/region to the column country/region as a share of the former's total exports.

and 11 per cent, respectively.[16] On the other hand, net importers of food, such as China, Mexico and Senegal, experience real consumption losses because of higher import prices.

The second channel is tightly linked to the first and has to do with the impact of countries' own policies. Thus, countries with high pre-reform tariffs or export taxes, such as Lithuania, Nigeria and North Africa, tend to experience larger

---

[16] The price increases are calculated using the Paasche price index, i.e. using the post-reform exports as weights for aggregating the prices of individual commodities. Unless explicitly noted, all price indices in this section are calculated using the Paasche formula. Price indices differ by country due to differences in the composition of exports (i.e. aggregation weights).

FIGURE 5
Most Countries Gain from the Removal of Agricultural Distortions

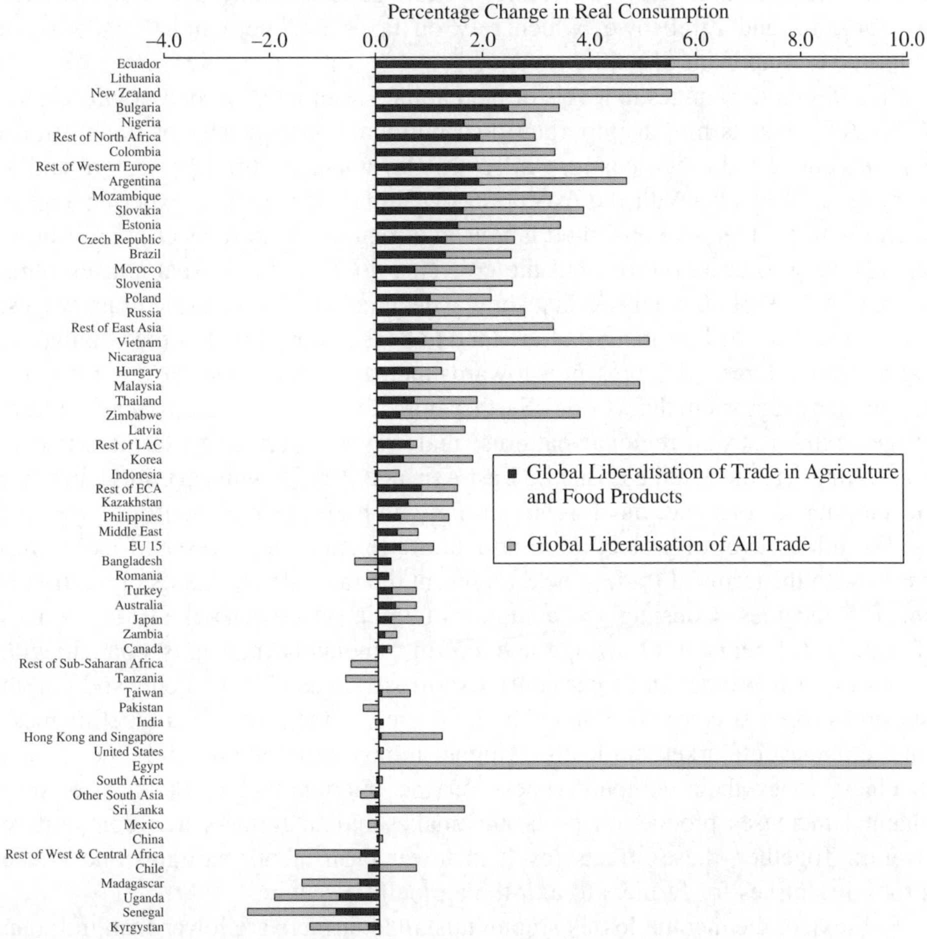

Percentage Change in Real Consumption

Notes:
The black bars show the percentage increase in consumption (at pre-reform prices) owing to the removal of trade distortions in agriculture and food products (excluding beverages and tobacco). The grey bars show the additional gains in consumption owing to the removal of all remaining trade barriers. The combined length of the two bars shows the consumption gains from a full global trade reform.

Source: Authors' simulations with the LINKAGE model.

consumption gains than countries where the initial distortions are low. If the initial trade barriers are sufficiently high, consumers may face lower post-reform prices of food even if import prices are rising; this is the case of North Africa, which experiences an increase in real consumption despite being a net food importer.

The third channel is the impact of trade reform on government budgets. Since the model does not include an explicit transversality condition, we maintain a fixed budget deficit closure, which means that any losses in public revenue (such as a reduction in tariff income) must be offset by a compensatory increase in the direct tax rate on the households.[17] Therefore, welfare gains are limited in countries such as Tanzania and Zimbabwe, which rely on taxes on international trade as an important component of public revenue.[18]

In addition to changes in levels of per capita consumption *across* countries, the LINKAGE results hint at important distributional consequences of trade reform *within* countries through changes in returns to labour in different sectors and at varying skill levels. With the exception of China, all countries experiencing an increase in payments to unskilled labour in agriculture also register consumption gains owing to trade reform, but the converse does not hold. Real consumption increases in 29 of 40 countries that show a decline in unskilled agriculture wages; since unskilled workers in agriculture tend to be the poorest part of the population, these results suggest that pressures towards increased inequality may be intensifying in many regions in the world.[19] Furthermore, the losses and gains in agriculture wages exhibit strong regional patterns: real wages of unskilled farmers rise in Latin America, the Middle East, and East Asia and Pacific, while declining in other developing regions and, much more strongly, in high-income countries.

The initial level of protection in agriculture (excluding processed food), combined with the terms of trade shock, represent the main determinants of the trends in farm incomes. Consider the example of India, where unskilled farm wages decline by 6.1 per cent following trade reform.[20] Indian farmers must contend with a loss of tariff protection (2 per cent), export subsidies (3.3 per cent) and output subsidies (6.9 per cent). The first channel decreases the farmers' competitiveness on the domestic market and leads to higher import penetration, while the second channel erodes their competitiveness on the international markets. The third channel increases production costs and makes Indian farmers less competitive overall. Together, these effects result in lower farm labour earnings and create strong incentives for farmers to exit the agriculture sector.

In Mexico, the income losses among unskilled farmers are lower than in India. This is partially attributable to its close trading relationship with the United States. Mexico purchases 75 per cent of its agriculture imports from the United States, whose export prices rise by 5.7 per cent because of the elimination of export and

---

[17] In other words, this closure choice gives rise to consistent measurement of household utility as the utility function does not include the consumption of public goods.

[18] In this situation, the ability of households to gain or lose from trade reform depends on (in addition to the impacts of the first two channels) their ability to substitute out of more expensive goods into cheaper alternatives.

[19] Note that trends in consumption per capita are unlikely to be representative of the welfare of agricultural households, since their weight in total consumption is low due to limited incomes and high incidence of poverty.

[20] The 6.1 per cent figure refers to change in the nominal wages. The change in real wages depends on the change of the CPI, which increases by 2 per cent relative to the base year.

production subsidies. Thus, the removal of agriculture price support in the United States puts upward pressure on import prices of agriculture in Mexico, which hurts consumers but increases the competitiveness of farmers on the domestic market. On the other hand, this trend is counteracted by the removal of tariff protection on agriculture (1.2 per cent) and output subsidies (0.8 per cent), which lead to a decrease in competitiveness of agriculture producers in Mexico and market share losses in both domestic and export markets.

Brazil, on the other hand, is an example of a country where a number of positive developments combine to produce a nearly 34 per cent gain in the wages of unskilled agriculture workers.[21] The import prices of agriculture in Brazil rise by 1.8 per cent, bolstering the domestic competitiveness of its farmers, while export prices increase by more than 10 per cent. Because Brazilian farmers do not receive any export or production subsidies, they are well positioned to take advantage of these opportunities and gain market share both domestically and abroad. Although some of the gains to agriculture producers are offset by the loss in domestic protection (import tariff of 2.4 per cent), Brazilian agriculture is still able to increase its production volume by 17.8 per cent following trade reform.

b. Microsimulation Results: Global Poverty and Inequality

In this section, we use the GIDD model and data to simulate the likely changes in global poverty and inequality because of the elimination of all agricultural trade distortions. Given the richness of the data and the numerous factors affecting global poverty and inequality within the GIDD, this section starts with two stylised simulations that illustrate, in a simple way, the expected effects of a global agricultural trade reform. Focusing only on low- and middle-income countries in our data, both these stylised simulations raise the *average* income in the developing world by 1 per cent. In the first instance, this occurs because of an increase in incomes of agricultural households only, while in the second exercise, the increase is due entirely to an expansion in non-agricultural incomes. The results of these two stylised simulations are shown with two growth incidence curves (GICs)[22] in Figure 6. The thin blue (Figure available in colour in the online version of the article) GIC captures the effects of assigning income gains only to agricultural households, while the thick red (Figure available in colour in the online version of the article) GIC raises incomes only for those households whose head works in non-agricultural activities. This simple exercise highlights the stark difference

---

[21] This is a nominal, not a real increase. Consumer prices in Brazil rise by 4 per cent following trade reform.

[22] The GIC is shows the changes in welfare along the entire income distribution, therefore capturing, in a single graph, the growth and distributional components of overall welfare changes. For a detailed description of the properties characterising the growth incidence curves, see Ravallion and Chen (2003).

FIGURE 6
Growth Incidence Curve of a 1 Per Cent Increase in Incomes

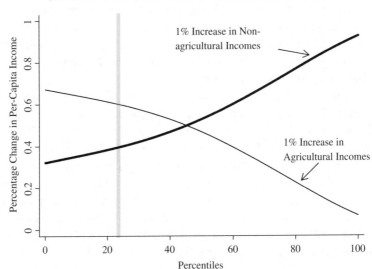

in the distributional consequences of these two shocks. The incidence of an increase in agricultural incomes is clearly progressive (the GIC is downward sloping) with the poorer quintile experiencing gains of about 0.6 per cent and the richer one gaining less than 0.2 per cent. Conversely, the incidence of an increase in non-agricultural incomes is regressive (the GIC is upward sloping) with the richer household benefiting more than poorer ones.

(i) Poverty and Inequality Impacts: A Global View

Translating the shocks from the LINKAGE model into poverty and inequality outcomes with the GIDD shows that the effects of a full removal of agricultural trade distortions on global poverty are close to zero. This limited impact is explained by several factors. First, the growth effects of the reform (i.e. changes in per capita consumption) are very small.

According to the GIDD, the world's average monthly household income increases 0.3 per cent after the removal of agricultural distortions, passing from an initial level of $207 to a final value of $208, 1993 PPP (see Table 4). Second, the reform has little impact on inequality at the global level. Although incomes rise in the agricultural and non-agricultural sectors alike, agricultural incomes increase by a little more than 1 per cent, while incomes in non-agricultural activities rise at 0.2 per cent. While this reduction in the non-agricultural income premium reduces inequality, Table 4 shows that income dispersion within the agricultural sector is also increasing, with the final change in global income

TABLE 4
Simulated Global Poverty and Inequality and Changes with Respect to Initial Levels

Strata	Gini (%)	Pop Shares (%)	Average Income	1-dollar Poverty Incidence (%)	Poverty Share (%)
Agricultural	44.9	44.8	65.4	31.7	75.9
Non-Agricultural	62.8	55.2	328.9	8.1	24.0
Total	67.0	100	210.8	18.7	100
Change with respect to the observed (simulated – observed)					
Agricultural	0.5	–	1.2*	0.87	1.02
Non-Agricultural	−0.2	–	0.2*	−0.36	−1.02
Total	−0.1	–	0.3*	0.18	–

Note:
*Changes in average income are expressed in percentage.

distribution being close to zero. The distributional changes taking place within the agricultural sector are such that the incidence of extreme poverty (under 1 dollar a day, PPP) in this sector rises by almost 1 percentage point as a consequence of the elimination of agricultural trade distortions. On the other hand, poverty among non-agricultural households experienced a reduction equal to 0.36 percentage points. The combination of poverty changes occurring in and out of the agricultural sector ends up increasing the number of individuals below the extreme poverty line by almost 10 million.

This result should be taken with caution since the poverty effect of the agricultural trade reform depends on where the poverty line is set. While global poverty measured by the 1-dollar-a-day poverty line shows a moderate increase of 0.18 percentage points (or 9.8 million additional poor) as a consequence of the reform, when measured at 2 dollars a day, poverty reduces by 0.3 percentage points (or 14.7 million less poor, see Table A1 in the Appendix).

The results presented so far have treated the world as a single entity, making no distinction between regions or countries. Thus, lack of major changes at the global level could be the outcome of offsetting trends between regions. As discussed in subsection 4a, farmers in many Latin America (LAC) countries are big winners from trade reform with an impressive increase of 16 per cent in their household income. By contrast, incomes of farmers in South Asia (SA) shrink more than 3 per cent after agricultural distortions are dismantled. To show the incidence of these changes among the population in the different regions, Figure 7 plots the GIC for Latin America, South Asia and the rest of the world. The GIC for Latin America shows that the agriculture-based growth in the region is highly pro-poor; on the contrary, South Asia's reduction in agricultural incomes is highly regressive, with the poorest households losing from the reform. East Asia and, to

FIGURE 7
Regional Growth Incidence Curves

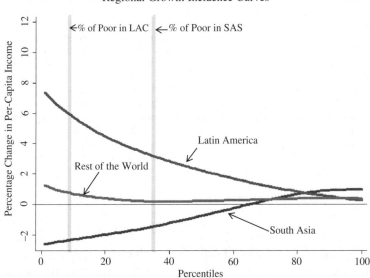

a lesser extent, sub-Saharan Africa benefit from the global reform, while the effects of the reform are progressive, albeit close to zero, for the rest of the world.

The differences in the reform outcomes across regions help explain the lack of significant change in global poverty. With half a billion people in extreme poverty, South Asia alone accounts for almost half of global poverty; on the other hand, Latin America contributes less than 5 per cent to global poverty (see Table 5). Hence, although removing agricultural distortions alleviates extreme poverty in most regions in the world, the increase in South Asia's head count ratio offsets these gains and drags an extra 9.8 million people below the poverty line. The results using the 2-dollar-per-day poverty line show a very different picture. Poverty is alleviated in all regions except for Middle East and North (see Table A1 in the Appendix). The results at the moderate poverty line are particularly interesting for South Asia, where agricultural trade reform becomes pro-poor instead of anti-poor as it was the case when using the 1-dollar-a-day PPP poverty line. This result is explained by the large number of non-agricultural households that are below the moderate poverty line in South Asia. South Asian households working in non-agricultural activities experience an increase in purchasing power after the agricultural markets are liberalised and therefore contribute to reduction in moderate poverty in the region.

(ii) Zooming in: Poverty and Inequality Effects Between and Within Countries
Global agricultural liberalisation has distributional and poverty effects that vary not only across regions but also between and within countries. This subsection

TABLE 5
Global and Regional Poverty

Region	Number of Poor (in Thousands)	Share of Global Poverty	Simulated Number of Poor (in Thousands)	Δ (Simulated – Observed)
East Asia	261,677	27.1	258,937	−2,740
Eastern Europe	3,607	0.4	3,576	−31
Latin America	40,075	4.1	37,677	−2,397
Middle East	1,614	0.2	1,544	−71
South Asia	466,165	48.3	481,350	15,185
Sub-Saharan Africa	192,555	19.9	192,461	−94
Global	965,693	100.0	975,545	9,851

Notes:
(1) Number of poor expressed in thousands.
(2) The simulations are based on the Global Income Distribution Dynamics's results.

summarises the poverty effects for each of the countries included in our sample and the distributional changes taking place within them. Table 5 shows that roughly 10 million individuals that would be pushed into poverty as a consequence of agricultural reform are the combination of a 15 million increase in poverty in South Asia and a 5 million decrease in poverty in the rest of the developing world. Figure 8 shows the countries that contribute the most to this reduction and increase in global poverty, respectively. Among the *new* poor, 85.2 per cent – almost 13 million – are Indian nationals, while 3.5 per cent are located in Bangladesh, and 2.1 per cent are Mexican. Although the increase in poverty is mainly an Indian phenomenon, all five South Asian countries contribute significantly to the global increase in poverty. On the other hand, the gross reduction in global poverty is distributed more evenly among the *winning* countries with the great majority of them being located in Latin America and East Asia and the Pacific (EAP). In fact, no country in EAP and only Chile and Mexico in LAC experience an increase in the number of extreme poor as a result of agricultural trade reform.

The contributions to the global entry and exit of poverty depicted in Figure 8 are, to a certain extent, the outcomes of differences in population size. For instance, a very populous country such as India can have a substantial contribution to global poverty without necessarily implying a large increase in the country's *head count ratio*. Another way of ranking countries in terms of their poverty outcomes is to consider the post-reform change in the head count ratio. Undertaking this exercise shows that, among countries where poverty falls, Peru's reduction of 3 percentage points in the head count ratio is, by far, the largest in the developing world. The incidence of poverty in Philippines and Ecuador decreases by 1.8 percentage points, just below the fall registered in Yemen and Paraguay (1.2). On the other hand, with an increase of 1.4 percentage points in the head count ratio, India is still the country with the largest increase in poverty. At the same time, as

FIGURE 8

Poverty Changes as a Proportion of the Total Change among the 10 Most Losing/Winning Countries

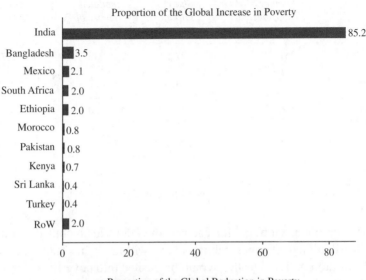

Proportion of the Global Increase in Poverty

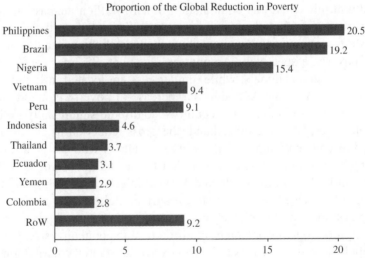

Proportion of the Global Reduction in Poverty

mentioned earlier, poverty in India falls by 0.3 percentage points if changes are evaluated at the 2-dollar-a-day poverty line. Interestingly, these changes in the head count ratio in India occur while average household income remains almost constant and are therefore entirely a result of a deterioration in income distribution.

Our results show that the significant increase in poverty in India is entirely explained by a post-reform increase in inequality of almost 1 Gini point. Three

FIGURE 9
Growth Incidence Curves for Brazil and India

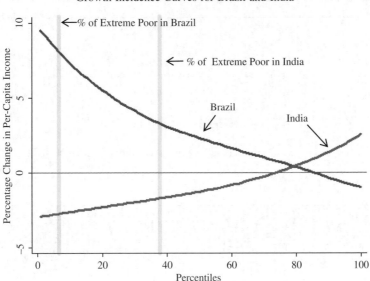

quarters of this increase are attributable to a rise in the agricultural-to non-agricultural income gap in India. On the other hand, poverty reduction in Brazil is the outcome of a combination of a 1 per cent increase in average income and a reduction in inequality of more than half a Gini point. The changes in overall growth and distribution taking place in India and Brazil are summarised by the GIC for these two countries plotted in Figure 9. Given the importance of Brazil and India in their respective regions, it is not surprising that the shape of the GIC for these countries are very similar to the GICs of their respective regions plotted in Figure 7. Figure 9 shows that the only beneficiaries of agricultural liberalisation in India are those in the top 22 per cent of the distribution; given than 83 per cent of the Indian population is below the 2-dollar-a-day poverty line, part of the top 22 per cent is formed by household under moderate poverty.

As we mentioned in Section 2, agricultural reforms can have important – agricultural to non-agricultural – real income distributional effects. Our results show that for most countries in our sample, removing agricultural distortions does not have large distributional effects. In more than half of the countries, the Gini coefficient shows a change of less than half a Gini point. This pattern is also observed in the changes in the country-specific Theil index plotted in Figure 10. There are distinguishable regional differences in the distributional effects of the reform, with countries in Latin America and East Asia experiencing a considerable reduction in income inequality while inequality in countries outside these regions remains constant or rises marginally. The advantage of using the Theil index as

FIGURE 10
Most of the Distributional Changes are Attributable to the Between Component

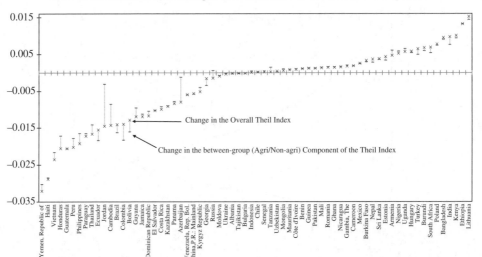

the inequality measure is that we can decompose its change into an effect attributable to shifts in the agricultural-to-non-agricultural wage gap (between effects)
and the effects as a result of income changes within these two groups. Figure 10
shows the total changes in the Theil index (depicted by a star) and the changes
attributable to movements in the non-agricultural income premium (little horizon-
tal bar). Since the 'between' effect is very close to the total distributional effect
for the majority of countries, we can conclude that the total change in income
distribution in these economies is mainly the outcome of changes in mean incomes
of the agricultural and non-agricultural sectors.

5. CONCLUSIONS AND POLICY MESSAGES

Trade distortions in agriculture and food represent the last major bastion of
protection and have proven to be the main point of contention in recent multilateral
trade negotiations. Using a newly developed data set and methodological approach
for evaluating the poverty and inequality effects of policy reforms – the GIDD
– this paper has evaluated the potential impacts of the removal of agriculture trade
distortions on the global income distribution.

There are three main messages emerging from our analysis. First, the liberalisation of agriculture and food markets is unlikely to have large effects on global
poverty. Our results show that the incidence of extreme poverty could rise by 0.2
per cent, while moderate poverty is likely to fall by 0.3 per cent.

The second message is that these small aggregate changes are produced by a combination of offsetting trends at the regional and country levels. With the elimination of all agriculture trade distortion, extreme poverty is reduced in all regions but in the Middle East and North Africa, where it is almost stable, and in South Asia, where it increases considerably. Since about 50 per cent of all poor people live in South Asia, the worsening of poverty in this region counterbalances all the gains in the other parts of the world and an additional 9 million people fall into poverty. At the moderate poverty line, 14 million people escape poverty and most regions benefit from lower poverty incidence with the exclusion of Eastern Europe and Central Asia and Middle East and North Africa. Many non-agriculture households in South Asia are clustered below the 2-dollar-a-day poverty line and trade reform-related improvement in their incomes, versus the agricultural incomes' decline, explain the difference in global poverty results when the 1-dollar- or the 2-dollar-a-day lines are used.

The third message is that the distributional changes because of agricultural trade reform are also likely to be mild, but exhibit a strong regional pattern. Inequality is likely to fall in regions such as Latin America, which are characterised by high initial inequality, and rise in regions like South Asia, characterised by low initial inequality. In addition, the decrease in inequality between agriculture and non-agriculture groups is offset by a higher within group inequality, which mainly originates from a widening of incomes within the agriculture sector. Inequality within countries varies within a wide interval ranging from increases of up to 3 Gini points to reduction of 2 Gini points. The majority of countries, around 60 per cent of those included in the sample, experience an increase of inequality.

These results suggest that allocative efficiency gains combined with distributional shifts originating from the removal of agriculture trade restrictions are not enough to significantly alleviate poverty at the 1-dollar-a-day threshold nor at a higher poverty line. The pattern of global incomes change triggered by such trade reform, as simulated by the model used in this paper, is complex and cannot be simplistically reduced to a boost in growth rates of agriculture. The latter remains an essential component in the strategy for poverty eradication, and trade liberalisation can only play a constructive but somewhat limited role.

There are several important caveats to our analysis. First, it should be emphasised that, although poverty reduction is a most worthy goal, it should not be the only, or even the first, metric with which to measure trade policy. Trade reform cannot be expected to benefit all constituents and can only do so in the presence of other complimentary policies. Second, our analysis is confined to examination of the effects of static efficiency gains only and does not consider the potential growth effects of trade liberalisation. Although our results show that the static gains from agriculture trade reform may not contribute to reduction in extreme poverty and may do little to combat moderate poverty, they do not imply that this pattern of trade liberalisation cannot be an effective tool for poverty reduction.

Finally, our micromodel considers only changes in labour income: while this is the most important income source for households at or near the poverty line, accounting for changes in other factor returns may yield results of a different magnitude.

APPENDIX

TABLE A1
Changes in Moderate Poverty

Region	Number of Poor (in Thousands)	Share of Global Poverty	Simulated Number of Poor (in Thousands)	Δ (Simulated – Observed)
East Asia	888,988	36.1	882,473	−6,515
Eastern Europe	42,194	1.7	41,641	−553
Latin America	104,573	4.2	100,044	−4,528
Middle East	11,425	0.5	11,720	294
South Asia	1,084,989	44.0	1,081,615	−3,374
Sub-Saharan Africa	331,264	13.4	331,203	−61
Global	2,463,434	100.0	2,448,696	−14,737

Note:
The simulations are based on the Global Income Distribution Dynamics's results.

REFERENCES

Anderson, Kym (2003), 'Trade Liberalization, Agriculture, and Poverty in Low-Income Countries', WIDER Discussion Paper No. 2003/05 (Helsinki: WIDER/UNU).
Anderson, Kym and Will Martin (2005), 'Agricultural Trade Reform and the Doha Development Agenda', The World Economy, **28**, 9, 1301–27.
Bourguignon, François and Luiz Pereira da Silva (eds.) (2003), The Impact of Economic Policies on Poverty and Income Distribution: Evaluation Techniques and Tools (New York: World Bank and Oxford University Press).
Bourguignon, F., V. Levin and D. Rosenblatt (2004), 'Declining International Inequality and Economic Divergence: Reviewing the Evidence through Different Lenses,' Economie Internationale, **100**, 4, 13–26.
Bussolo, Maurizio, Rafael De Hoyos, Denis Medvedev and Dominique van der Mensbrugghe (2007), 'Global Growth and Distribution: Are China and India Reshaping the World?' World Bank Policy Research Working Paper 4392 (Washington, DC: World Bank).
Bussolo, M., R. De Hoyos and D. Medvedev (2009), 'Global Income Distribution and Poverty in the Absence of Agricultural Distortions', Policy Research Working Paper #4849 (Washington, DC: World Bank).
Bussolo, M., R. De Hoyos and D. Medvedev (2010), 'Economic Growth and Income Distribution: Linking Macroeconomic Models with Household Survey Data at the Global Level', The International Journal of Microsimulation, **3**, 1, 92–103.
Chen, Shaohua and Martin Ravallion (2003), 'Household Welfare Impacts of China's Accession to the World Trade Organization', Policy Research Working Paper 3040 (Washington, DC: World Bank).

Ferreira, Francisco H. G. and Phillippe G. Leite (2003), 'Meeting the Millennium Development Goals in Brazil: Can Microsimulations Help?' *Economía*, **3**, 2, 235–79.

Ferreira, Francisco H. G. and Phillippe G. Leite (2004), 'Educational Expansion and Income Distribution: A Microsimulation for Ceará', in Anthony Shorrocks and Rolph van der Hoeven (eds.), *Growth, Inequality and Poverty* (London: Oxford University Press), 222–50.

Hoekman, B., F. Ng and M. Olarreaga (2002), '*Reducing Agriculture Tariffs Versus Domestic Support: What's More Important for Developing Countries?*' *CEPR Discussion Papers 3576* (London: CEPR).

Krueger, Anne O., Maurice Schiff and Alberto Valdés (eds.) (1991), *The Political Economy of Agricultural Pricing Policy* (Washington, DC: World Bank).

McCulloch, N., L. A. Winters and X. Cirera (2002), *Trade Liberalization and Poverty: A Handbook* (London: DfID and CEPR).

van der Mensbrugghe, Dominique (2005), *The LINKAGE Model Technical Documentation* (Washington, DC: World Bank).

Nicita, A. (2004), 'Who Benefited from Trade Liberalization in Mexico? Measuring the Effects on Household Welfare', *World Bank Policy Research* Working Paper 3265.

Ravallion, M. and S. Chen (2003), 'Measuring Pro-Poor Growth', *Economics Letters*, **78**, 1, 93–99.

Rodrik, D. (1998) 'Why Is Trade Reform So Difficult in Africa?' *Journal of African Economies*, **7**, 1, 10–36.

Winters, L.A. (2000), '*Trade, Trade Policy and Poverty: What are the Links?*', Center for Economic Policy Research, Discussion Paper 2382 (London: CEPR).

4

Agricultural Export Subsidies and Domestic Support Reform under the WTO System: What Does It Mean for Welfare in West Africa?

John Alexander Nuetah, Ting Zuo and Xin Xian

1. INTRODUCTION

*T*HERE has been increasing debates in recent years about the impacts of developed countries' agricultural support policies on producers' welfare in developing and least developed countries (LDCs). Producers in developing countries and LDCs, including those in West Africa, complain that agricultural support policies in industrialised countries distort world market prices of agricultural commodities. These price distortions are said to be negatively affecting the economic welfare of LDCs and developing countries' producers of agricultural commodities. Also, some development institutions and organisations have further complained that farm policies in developed nations contribute to poverty and livelihood destruction in Third World countries. For instance, Oxfam (2004) argued that European Union agricultural subsidies encourage overproduction and drive down world prices of key commodities, such as sugar, dairy products and cereals, and destroy livelihoods in developing countries. In addition, Nebehay (2006) further affirms that these subsidies are destroying African agriculture and exacerbating

The authors acknowledge and extend sincere thanks and appreciations to the anonymous referee of *The World Economy* for the insightful comments, criticisms and suggestions that helped improve the content and structure of this paper.

the continent's hunger problems, thereby depriving it of the opportunity to reach a minimum living standard. Jensen and Zobbe (2006) then called for a reduction in developed countries' domestic supports to level the playing field of the agricultural commodity market.

This growing public outcry in both developed and developing countries strengthened the negotiations of agricultural trade policy reform initiated by the World Trade Organization (WTO) during the Uruguay Rounds, and discussions continued under the Doha Development Agenda (DDA). Negotiations under the DDA are centred on the creation of market access for agricultural products from LDCs and developing countries, elimination of agricultural export subsidies and reduction in domestic support in both developed and developing economies. Preliminary agreement reached at this negotiation termed the 'July Framework for Establishing Modalities in Agriculture' subjects developed countries' domestic support termed as 'trade-distorting' to deeper cuts. The Doha Ministerial Declaration further called for a reduction of, with a view to phasing out, all forms of export subsidies in both developed and developing countries by 2013 (WTO, 2004).

However, there remain uncertainties among policymakers and researchers about the welfare impacts of the proposed DDA reforms on LDCs and developing countries. For instance, Anderson and Martin (2006) argue that most LDCs lack market for most commodities and so have nothing to gain if market access is granted. They further assert that the benefit of such reforms will accrue only to large developing countries who are major exporters. Hertel and Keeney (2006) also argue that the price rises resulting from agricultural trade reforms will lead to welfare gain for net food exporting countries but net food importers will be losers. They further emphasise that most developing countries will experience terms-of-trade losses if agricultural tariffs, domestic supports and export subsidies were to be eliminated by high-income countries. Other research findings also indicate that consumers in middle income and net food importing low-income countries will be losers (e.g. Baker, 2006; Peters, 2006; Anderson, 2009).

Another basis for the inclusion of agriculture into world trade negotiation is its assumed poverty reduction prospects for poor countries. Some researchers, for instance, Frith (2005), Anderson and Valenzuela (2007), and Binswanger-Mkhize and McCalla (2008), argue that agricultural trade reforms will create an opportunity for the producers in low-income countries to lift themselves out of poverty. On the contrary, however, others (e.g. Panagariya, 2004; Anderson et al., 2006a, 2006b; Hoekman and Messerlin, 2006; Hertel et al., 2007, 2008), counter-argue that eliminating agricultural export subsidies in developed countries is not poverty-friendly because subsidies reduce food prices and that many poor and net food importing countries who depend on these subsidised commodities will be losers.

The foregoing suggests there remain major disagreements over the welfare impacts of agricultural policy reforms. Nevertheless, while these studies provide useful insights into the impacts of these proposed reforms on LDCs and developing countries in general, none of the reviewed literature has specifically studied the welfare impacts of these reforms on West African nations. That is, most of these studies are focused either globally or continentally. For example, Hertel and Keeney's (2006) work on sub-Saharan Africa concludes that the continent will experience total welfare loss from all expects of agricultural trade liberalisation. But Summer's (2006) analysis of the effect of US cotton subsidies on cotton prices and the implications for four African countries (Benin, Burkina Faso, Chad and Mali) concludes that eliminating such subsidies would result in increases in farm prices of seed cotton, which would then increase the gross and net incomes of cotton producers in West Africa. Such finding presents a firm case for eliminating cotton subsidies in the United States to increase the welfare of cotton producers in the region. However, it falls short of expressing the welfare losses cotton farmers (who are also consumers of other subsidised commodities) will experience importing other US commodities (such as US rice and maize) which are also required under DDA for export subsidies elimination. This study, thus, adopting a wide range of agricultural commodities focuses specifically on analysing the potential welfare impacts West Africa tends to experience if domestic support were reformed and export subsidies eliminated according to the July Framework agreement of the DDA.[1] West Africa is a region that comprises 16 countries. We however base our analysis on 15 of these countries on which WTO data are available.

Our analysis of domestic support and export subsidies is based on two main reasons. First, except for three countries in the region (Ivory Coast, Ghana and Nigeria) which have developing countries status under the WTO arrangement, the rest are LDCs that are basically net importers of agricultural commodities. In accordance with the July Framework, all LDCs are exempted from tariff cuts, and so, market access creation through tariff reduction is unlikely to make any major impact on tariff revenues of most of these countries. So, the welfare impacts to be felt by these countries will most likely result directly from export subsidies and domestic support since they directly affect the prices of agricultural commodities. For instance, subsidies on cotton, maize and rice as percentage of producer prices in the United States from 1999 to 2005 constituted 58, 72 and 25 per cent, respectively, while in all other OCED countries, it represented 81 and 29 per cent, respectively, for rice and maize (Schnepf and Womach, 2006, 2007) during the

---

[1] The 28 commodities analysed are grouped into the following categories: livestock; meat – (bovine meat, sheep meet, pig meat and poultry); dairy products – (concentrated milk, cheese, and butter); grains – (wheat, rice, maize, barley and sorghum); vegetables – (pulse and potatoes); fruits – (apples, citrus fruits, bananas and other tropical fruits); sugar – (raw sugar and refined sugar); beverages – (green coffee, processed coffee, cocoa beans and processed cocoa); cotton and vegetable oils.

same period.[2] These subsidies lowered the export prices of these commodities at the advantage of net importers. For example, between 1990 and 2003, it cost on average $393.48 to grow and mill one metric ton of white rice in the United States but the same quantity was exported for $329.44 per metric ton. Similarly, a metric ton of maize was produced in the United States during the same period at an average cost of $129.94 but exported for $110.94. These low export prices made US produced rice and maize to be sold at prices about 16.27 and 14.62 per cent, respectively, cheaper than the cost of production.[3]

Second, most of the agricultural commodities subsidised in developed countries are major dietary commodities for almost all West African nations. Despite the dietary importance of these commodities, however, their domestic demands far exceed domestic supplies. Rice, for example, sustains the livelihoods of over 100 million people in the region (Diagne, 2008), with average per capita consumption from 2000 to 2007 ranging from a minimum of 61.64 to a maximum of 79.93 kg/ annum. However, average minimum and maximum per capita productions during the period was lower than per capita requirement – 32.29 and 41.20 kg/annum, respectively.[4] West Africa is thus a net consumer of these commodities along with all the other commodities considered in this paper. Therefore, analysing the impact of the liberalisation of these aspects of agricultural trade on West Africa will provide useful insight for policymakers in the region to formulate or adopt the necessary policy strategies to ameliorate any potentially adverse impacts.

Our approach is somehow different from previous works because none of the reviewed literatures has carried out such a comprehensive welfare analysis for West African countries. Furthermore, our analysis is significant because it tries to quantify the potential gains (losses) individual WTO member country of the region will encounter from agricultural trade reforms under DDA. It further endeavours to provide West African policymakers an insight into the potentially adverse effects of such reforms to enable them formulate relevant policies to ameliorate the situation. In addition, unlike other studies that have mainly used data in Global Trade Analysis Project (GTAP) database for analysis, ours uses data from the Agricultural Trade and Policies Simulation Model (ATPSM) database.

We organise the rest of this paper into three sections. Section 2 discusses the methodology and the data sources. In Section 3, we provide the results of the

---

[2] Rice, maize and cotton are important commodities for the economies of West Africa. Rice and maize are major staples while cotton is a major economic crop for a few countries. So, subsidies or its removal tends to either positively or negatively effect livelihoods in the region.
[3] These production costs and export prices were calculated from data provided in work done by Murphy et al. (2005). This work provides detailed information on production cost and export prices of five major agricultural commodities produced and trade by the US between 1990 and 2003.
[4] These figures were calculated from FAOSTAT data on productions and consumptions of these commodities in the selected countries.

analysis beginning with a presentation of changes in world prices and consumer and producer surpluses as well as the net national welfare changes per individual West African country. We then compare these results with two groups of three selected developed and developing countries. In the final section, we present the conclusion along with food security implications and policy suggestions.

2. METHODOLOGY AND DATA

In this paper, we use the updated version (version 3.1) of the ATPSM to analyse the potential economic welfare impacts West Africa will experience from domestic agricultural support and export subsidies reforms in developed and developing countries. ATPSM is a static, partial-equilibrium, global agricultural trade model developed by the United Nations Conference on Trade and Agricultural Development (UNCTAD) and the Food and Agriculture Organization (FAO) to estimate the potential economic effects of changes in within-quota, applied and out-quota tariffs, import quotas, export subsidies and domestic support on production, consumption, prices, trade flows, trade revenues, quota rents, producer and consumer surplus, and welfare. In this study, however, our target is to assess the potential welfare impact of reforming domestic agricultural support and export subsidies based on the July Framework scenario. This scenario is based on a tiered formula that adopts a Harbinson approach plus sensitive and special product provisions.

Tiered formula classifies tariffs into various bands for subsequent reduction from bound rates and ensures that tariffs in higher tiers have larger cuts than those in lower ones. Harbinson, in his revised version of the modalities on agricultural trade reform, tries to harmonise tariff structure by having a more progressive schedule where larger tariff cuts are mandated for higher tariff rates, with different levels of tariff reduction set for developed and developing countries (see Table 1).

The model further adopts the 'sensitive products' preferential tariff treatment provisions made by the reform modalities for both developed and developing countries and the 'special product' provision for developing countries. Sensitive products are commodities deemed by a country essential for political stability. Under the 'sensitive product' provision, developed nations are allowed to treat 4 to 6 per cent of their dutiable commodities (in instances where less than 30 per cent of their tariff lines are below the top band) and up to 6 to 8 per cent (where more than 30 per cent of their tariff lines are in the top band) as 'sensitive products' (WTO, 2007). Reduction in tariff on developed countries' 'sensitive products' range from a minimum of 1/3 to a maximum of 2/3 of the requirement mandated under the tiered formula. On the other hand, developing countries are allowed to designate about 5.2 to 7.8 per cent of their dutiable commodities as 'sensitive products' (where less than 30 per cent of their tariff lines fall within the highest

TABLE 1
Harbinson's Tariff Reduction Formula for Developed and Developing Countries

Tariff Rates	Average Reduction (%)	Minimum Cut (%)
Developed countries		
Ad valorem rates >90%	60	45
Ad valorem rates between 15% and 90%	50	35
Ad valorem rates <15%	40	25
Developing countries		
Ad valorem rates >120%	40	30
Ad valorem rates between 60% and 120%	35	20
Ad valorem rates between 20% and 60%	20	15
Ad valorem rates <20%	25	15

Source: Revised Harbinson's modalities for further commitment, 2007.

band) and 8 to 10.6 per cent when more than 30 per cent of the dutiable tariff lines fall within the top band. These countries are obligated to a minimum reduction of 1/3 and a maximum of 2/3 of the reduction required under the tiered formula. Furthermore, developing countries are allowed to treat as 'special products' (SP products), agricultural products of particular importance to food security, livelihood security and rural development. Commodities that qualify for SP-product treatment are subject to simple average reduction rate of 10 per cent with a minimum cut of 5 per cent per tariff line. With regard to export subsidies rate, the parameter assumed for the cut is 100 per cent for both developed and developing countries, while the rate of reduction adopted for domestic support is 60 and 40 per cent, respectively, for developed and developing countries.

For the purpose of our analysis, this study selects 28 of the 35 ATPSM agricultural commodities and separates them into 10 subgroups and individual commodities – livestock, meat, dairy products, grain, vegetables, fruits, sugar, beverages, cotton and vegetable oils. We then simulate the welfare changes for both producers and consumers in the selected countries and calculate the total net welfare changes. We measure welfare change in terms of changes in consumer surplus and producer surplus and consider the total welfare impact resulting from the policy reform as the net of changes in consumer surplus (ΔCS) and producer surplus (ΔPS).

$$\Delta W = \Delta CS + \Delta PS. \tag{1}$$

ΔCS is measured as the product of change in consumer price (ΔP_{c}) and consumer demand (D) plus half the change in domestic demand (ΔD_{d})

$$\Delta CS = -\Delta P_{\mathrm{c}}\left[D + 0.5\left(\Delta D_{\mathrm{d}}\right)\right]. \tag{2}$$

while ΔPS is considered as the product of change in producer price (ΔP_p) and supply (S) plus half the change in domestic supply (ΔS_d), plus the change in quota rent captured by exporting producers ($c\Delta U$),

$$\Delta PS = \Delta P_p \left[S + 0.5(\Delta S_d) \right] + c\Delta U. \tag{3}$$

To determine whether West Africa which comprises mainly LDCs whose welfare concerns are used as the basis for the argument for agricultural trade reforms will gain or lose from the reforms, we compare the welfare change of West Africa with three of the large developing countries (Brazil, China and India) who are accused of exercising punitive tariffs while themselves subsidise and produce both for export and for domestic consumption, and three developed countries (the EU, Japan and United States) who are the major subsidisers and exporters of these commodities.[5] The results indicate that West African nations will all be losers, while the developed and large developing countries will be gainers.

Data used in this study were gathered from two sources. Production and consumption panel data from the FAO statistical database (FAOSTAT) were used to calculate per capita production and consumption based on the total population of the selected West African countries. Consumption figures were calculated as the difference between the sum of domestic production, national import and food aid, and the quantity of national export. The mean data used for welfare analysis are macrolevel data submitted to the WTO by member countries on the level of subsidies and tariffs used in their agricultural sectors. These data were compiled by the FAO and UNCTAD and are available in the ATPSM model for use.

As others who have used the model (e.g. Vanzetti and Graham, 2002; Peters, 2006), alert, however, a major limitation of the model is the quality and reliability of the data. The data quality is particularly an issue since there are many commodities and countries to deal with. Furthermore, the data reliability is a major problem because information on applied rates and other official supports may not have been accurately notified to the WTO. Although these limitations may render the results imperfect, these data, however, provide necessary information for calculating changes in economic welfare resulting from agricultural policy reform according the DDA negotiation. Thus, results of this analysis provide useful insights into the potential welfare impacts of agricultural trade reform on West Africa.

3. POTENTIAL WELFARE IMPACTS

In this section, we discuss the potential impacts of the proposed DDA agricultural trade reforms on West Africa. We consider the effects on world agricultural commodity prices, as well as on consumers and producers in countries considered

---

[5] The EU refers to the original 15 Member States of the European Union.

in the study. We begin with discussion of the impacts on world prices of agricultural commodities and then continue with discussion of the potential welfare effects on West Africa and the selected groups of developed and large developing countries.

a. Effects of Changes in World Prices

As net importers, the potential welfare impacts of the reforms on West Africa will result mainly from changes in the world market prices of the commodities analysed. As can be seen in Table 2, the prices of some of the main agricultural outputs of the LDCs (coffee, green and cocoa beans) which are mainly raw material for the developed nations' industries will fall, while the prices of the finished products of these commodities (which are imported by these LDCs) will rise.

In addition, there will be a net increase in the world prices of all the essential commodities consumed by the region. Although these price increases will create different effects on consumers and producers in the different countries in the region, the net national impacts will be negative.

b. Changes in Consumer Surplus

In Table 3, we present changes in consumer surplus for the countries analysed. These results indicate that West African consumers will experience total net welfare loss of about $591.93 million from the consumption of the commodities analysed. Except for livestock whose consumption in a few producing countries is expected to yield consumer surplus, consumers of all other commodities in the 15 West African countries will encounter consumer losses. The largest aggregate losses will be incurred from commodities categorised as fruits, grains, dairy products, meat, vegetables and sugar. This indicates the dietary importance of these commodities to the region. On the other hand, West African consumers experience a potential net welfare gain of approximately $5.59 million from trade in livestock. The net welfare gains by livestock consumers in the West African region result from the fall in the world market price of livestock as a result of the proposed trade policy reforms. As shown in Table 2, the price of a metric ton of livestock is expected to fall by US$1.05. These potential gains accrue to eight of the 15 countries considered with three of these being the only countries in the region with developing country status under the WTO. Although there is also expected to be a net fall in the world market prices of green coffee and cocoa beans, consumers will encounter net welfare losses in the beverage categories since the processed forms of these products, which they mainly imported, will experience price rises.

Like consumers in West Africa, those in the three large developing countries used for comparison will also encounter welfare gains from trade in livestock.

TABLE 2
Changes in the World Prices of Commodities Analysed (US$/metric ton)

Commodities	Initial World Price	Final World Price	Change in World Price
Livestock	1,265.67	1,264.61	−1.05
Meat			
Bovine meat	1,966.00	2,048.45	82.45
Sheep meat	2,713.67	2,762.70	49.03
Pig meat	1,213.33	1,290.87	77.53
Poultry	1,345.33	1,395.40	50.06
Dairy products			
Milk, conc.	1,766.67	2,125.39	358.73
Butter	1,276.00	1,425.86	149.86
Cheese	1,902.00	2,167.18	265.18
Grains			
Wheat	121.33	129.12	7.80
Rice	208.67	211.72	3.05
Barley	82.33	90.50	8.16
Maize	111.33	113.69	2.36
Sorghum	89.00	90.74	1.74
Vegetables			
Pulses	529.33	536.30	6.96
Tomatoes	820.00	835.87	15.87
Fruits			
Apples	548.33	565.97	17.63
Citrus fruits	470.00	479.62	9.62
Bananas	477.00	482.40	5.40
Other tropical fruits	735.33	745.69	10.36
Beverages			
Coffee, green	1,417.00	1,408.42	−8.60
Coffee, proc.	4,763.87	4,876.38	112.51
Cocoa beans	1,039.00	1,037.94	−1.06
Cocoa, proc.	1,676.00	1,740.08	64.08
Tea	2,262.00	2,318.17	56.17
Sugar			
Sugar, raw	252.66	257.06	4.39
Sugar, refined	321	337.29	16.29
Vegetable oils	254	258.75	4.75
Cotton	1,178.33	1,178.65	0.31

Source: Agricultural Trade and Policies Simulation Model simulation results.

However, they will all experience net consumer losses from the other commodities. Consumers in China will encounter the biggest loss (about $5 billion) followed by India (about $2.75 billion) and Brazil. These results validate other research findings (e.g. Baker, 2006; Peters, 2006; Anderson, 2009), that consumers in developing and LDCs will be the main losers from global agricultural trade policy reforms. This therefore implies that these consumers will experience more economic hardship, especially those in the net food importing countries of West Africa.

TABLE 3

Change in Consumer Surplus ($million) for (A) West African Countries, Selected (B) Large Developing Countries, and (C) Developed Countries

Country	Livestock	Meat	Dairy Product	Grains	Vegetables	Fruits	Sugar	Beverages	Cotton	Vegetable Oils	Net Consumer Surplus
(A)											
Benin	0.00	−5.35	−5.98	−3.04	−3.54	−1.21	−0.46	−0.14	−0.04	−0.23	−20.00
Burkina Faso	0.23	−2.03	−0.48	−3.59	−2.68	−0.06	−0.41	−0.05	−0.02	−0.19	−9.26
Gambia	0.00	−0.54	−4.35	−0.99	−0.36	−0.01	−4.27	−0.33	0.00	−0.52	−11.36
Ghana	0.12	−4.43	−4.78	−7.23	−4.28	−3.59	−2.96	−1.08	−0.05	−0.97	−29.21
Guinea	0.00	−1.18	−4.12	−4.45	−0.82	−5.00	−3.50	−1.08	0.00	−0.79	−20.94
Guinea Bissau	0.00	−1.15	−0.21	−0.34	−0.03	−0.39	−0.06	−0.01	0.00	−0.12	−2.31
Ivory Coast	3.35	−5.28	−7.56	−10.19	−2.03	−0.26	−3.99	−2.36	−0.07	−0.52	−28.92
Liberia	0.00	−1.05	−0.46	−0.68	−0.08	−0.95	−0.24	−0.00	0.00	−0.25	−3.71
Mali	0.00	−5.89	−5.65	−5.29	−1.79	−0.41	−3.91	−1.33	0.00	−0.50	−24.82
Mauritania	0.13	−0.42	−3.67	−2.21	−0.37	−0.38	−4.17	−0.40	0.00	−0.14	−11.62
Niger	0.17	−1.65	−8.76	−1.54	−4.62	−0.19	−1.19	−0.20	0.00	−0.17	−18.15
Nigeria	1.33	−46.94	−32.90	−65.90	−56.34	−117.94	−24.80	−1.66	−0.04	−14.54	−359.75
Senegal	0.22	−7.19	−10.57	−7.70	−0.69	−3.53	−3.78	−1.11	0.00	−1.07	−35.42
Sierra Leone	0.00	−1.25	−0.83	−1.17	−0.95	−1.21	−0.43	−0.03	0.00	−0.35	−6.23
Togo	0.03	−1.73	−3.12	−2.94	−0.60	−0.15	−0.76	−0.68	−0.05	−0.26	−10.27
West Africa	5.59	−86.09	−93.42	−117.27	−79.20	−135.29	−54.94	−10.46	−0.23	−20.61	−591.93
(B)											
Brazil	16.49	−668.76	−172.41	−182.77	−72.46	−298.00	−539.00	−42.94	−0.19	−14.86	−1,975.82
China	34.62	−2,106.95	−98.19	−1,771.83	−356.48	−511.00	−171.00	−18.99	−1.68	−1.62	−5,003.04
India	10.82	−148.18	−344.37	−845.36	−269.72	−276.91	−747.00	−46.50	−0.83	−85.83	−2,753.57
(C)											
EU	166.17	5,581.11	7,105.44	3,543.79	582.36	1,964.45	4,068.44	17,264.49	−0.45	21.34	40,297.16
Japan	180.11	3,684.35	463.61	1,581.92	1,293.87	244.67	1,954.26	5,538.33	−0.08	3.58	14,944.62
United States	38.25	−1,744.02	−481.83	−811.73	−13.54	−48.23	−110.03	−1,465.36	3.94	−27.03	−4,659.59

Source: Authors' calculation from agricultural trade and policy simulation model (ATSPM) simulation results.

For the developed nations in our analysis, only consumers in the United States will experience net consumer losses. But those in Japan and the EU will experience net consumer surpluses. The biggest gainers among consumers in the developed countries will be in the EU with the largest surpluses being accumulated from the consumption of beverages, dairy products, meat, sugar and grains. The large consumer surplus in the EU after policy reform is due apparently to the existence of a heavily protected agricultural commodity market which raises prices for consumers in favour of producers. For consumers in the United States, the only potential welfare gains will be experienced from trade in cotton and livestock. But because these gains are insufficient to compensate the losses encountered from the consumption of the other commodities, US consumers, like those in West Africa and the selected large developed countries, will also end up as net losers. In Japan, however, consumers will end up as net gainers with the largest gains deriving from the consumption of beverages, meat and sugar.

c. Changes in Producer Surplus

The potential producer surpluses that West African producers and producers in our selected countries will encounter from domestic support reduction and export subsidies elimination are presented in Table 4. The results in Table 4A indicate that producers in West Africa are expected to gain from implementation of the DDA. As shown, all the region's producers would experience welfare gains from the commodities analysed except for livestock producers. The net potential welfare gain for the region is about $423.78 million, even though livestock farmers are expected to experience losses of about $5.43 million. The largest contributions to producers' gains will come from fruits, meat, vegetables and grains, while cotton contributes the least to net producer surplus – even for the main cotton producers in the region.[6]

As with West Africa, producers in the large developing countries will enjoy welfare gains (except for livestock producers), while the largest share of net producer surpluses will be accumulated from meat, grains, sugar, and fruits. As shown in Table 4B, China is expected to experience the largest producer surplus (about $5.08 billion) followed by India (about $2.82 billion) and Brazil (about $2.21 billion). This result is in accord with Hertel et al.'s (2008) argument that reforming developed countries' agricultural policies would lift large members of developing country farm households out of poverty, but impoverish net-food importers.

However, unlike producers in West Africa and the selected large developing countries, most producers in the developed nations will be losers (see Table 4C). In the EU and Japan, producers of cotton will experience welfare gains, while

---

[6] The main cotton producers in West Africa are Benin, Burkina Faso and Mali.

TABLE 4

Change in Consumer Surplus ($million) for (A) West African Countries, Selected (B) Large Developing Countries, and (C) Developed Countries

Country	Livestock	Meat	Dairy Product	Grains	Vegetables	Fruits	Sugar	Beverages	Cotton	Vegetable Oils	Net Producer Surplus
(A)											
Benin	0.00	1.50	0.06	2.25	3.21	1.02	0.10	0.00	0.08	0.20	8.40
Burkina Faso	-0.24	2.07	0.21	3.53	2.70	0.14	0.59	0.00	0.04	0.22	9.25
Gambia	0.00	0.25	0.00	0.38	0.04	0.01	0.00	0.01	0	0.31	1.01
Ghana	-0.12	3.46	0.17	3.72	4.05	4.25	0.77	3.92	0.01	0.90	21.14
Guinea	0.00	1.10	0.05	2.15	0.55	5.07	0.55	0.79	0.00	0.67	10.93
Guinea Bissau	0.00	1.13	0.00	0.29	0.02	0.40	0.00	0.00	0.00	0.01	1.92
Ivory Coast	-3.20	4.12	0.24	3.82	1.89	3.12	1.95	14.07	0.07	0.78	26.84
Liberia	0.00	0.77	0.00	0.30	0.04	0.95	0.09	-0.03	0.00	0.22	2.34
Mali	0.00	5.94	0.05	3.64	1.72	0.35	0.54	0.01	0.00	0.45	12.70
Mauritania	-0.13	0.26	0.95	0.32	0.31	0.33	1.43	0.00	0.00	0.01	3.48
Niger	-0.21	1.67	5.13	1.21	4.67	0.09	0.39	0.01	0.00	0.08	13.04
Nigeria	-1.28	46.9	9.02	41.44	56.05	120	3.26	1.12	0.05	13.67	289.77
Senegal	-0.22	6.78	0.31	0.96	0.66	3.33	1.70	0.02	0.00	0.84	14.38
Sierra Leone	0.00	1.08	0.00	0.68	0.88	1.18	0.04	-0.08	0.00	0.31	4.08
Togo	-0.03	1.55	0.00	1.70	0.45	0.15	0.03	0.42	0.07	0.16	4.50
West Africa	-5.43	78.57	16.19	66.39	77.24	139.95	11.39	20.27	0.31	18.91	423.78
(B)											
Brazil	-16.47	760.42	153.16	124.45	73.33	330.18	705.51	58.20	0.21	22.32	2,211.31
China	-34.60	2,144.33	84.53	1,775.91	367.44	541.85	154.65	39.16	1.63	2.70	5,077.62
India	-10.78	166.62	361.82	890.30	251.42	278.84	769.21	58.63	0.69	48.26	2,815.02
(C)											
EU	-136.46	-11,850.25	-12,105.81	-6,788.25	-515.70	-1,383.57	-7,167.85	45.38	0.22	-13.82	-39,916.10
Japan	-166.95	-3,385.77	-808.47	-278.15	-68.02	-155.87	-1,170.93	-81.29	0.00	-2.52	-6,117.98
United States	-37.28	2,029.50	-1,781.68	806.82	42.18	88.33	-539.27	103.64	-1.44	31.78	742.57

Source: Authors' calculation from ATSPM simulation results.

those in the United States will be losers. Nevertheless, US producers of meat, grains, vegetables, fruits and beverages will be gainers. Furthermore, the United States will enjoy net producer surplus, while the EU and Japan will encounter net producer losses. The high level of producer losses in these developed nations can be attributed to the apparent existence of high level of domestic support and trade protectionism. For instance, the percentage of producer support estimates in Japan and the EU from 1993 to 2004 averaged 58 and 35, respectively (Kwiecinski, 2008). This indicates that producers in these countries are protected by domestic agricultural policies.

d. Changes in Total Welfare

Table 5 presents the changes in total welfare for the selected countries. As stated earlier, total welfare change is the net of changes in consumer and producer surpluses. The figures in Table 5A indicate that all countries in West Africa will be net losers of agricultural trade reform under the DDA arrangement. Even though a great majority of the producers tend to experience welfare gains, these potential gains are insufficient to offset the losses to be encountered by consumers. The region is therefore expected to encounter a total net welfare loss of approximately $168.16 million. Except for livestock trade where a few countries (Ghana, Ivory Coast, Mauritania, Nigeria, Senegal and Togo), and cotton where most countries will enjoy some minimum net welfare gains, all countries in the region will experience net welfare losses in trade in almost all of the other commodities.

For the major cotton producers, the gains from cotton are insufficient to compensate for losses from other commodities so they all end up as net losers. Thus, although the arguments that US cotton subsidy is destroying livelihoods in cotton producing countries in West Africa (e.g. Oxfam, 2004; Summer, 2006), and that its removal would improve net welfare in cotton producing countries in the region and lift them out of poverty is acceptable to some extent, nevertheless, because these producers themselves depend on the consumption of other commodities which are produced in subsidising countries, the expected net welfare gains by these countries will have minimum poverty reducing effects. This indicates that export subsidies elimination and domestic support reduction as proposed under the DDA are currently not in the best interest of West African nations as the region will become poorer with such reform rather than the glamorous picture painted by agricultural trade reform advocates.

There is, however, great prospect for the large developing countries to gain from agricultural trade reforms. The results in Table 5B show that these countries will all become winners from reducing domestic support and eliminating export subsidies.

Although some will experience losses in some of the commodities analysed, they will all end up as winners with Brazil enjoying the biggest gain (about

TABLE 5

Change in Consumer Surplus ($million) for (A) West African Countries, Selected (B) Large Developing Countries, and (C) Developed Countries

Country	Livestock	Meat	Dairy Products	Grains	Vegetables	Fruits	Sugar	Beverages	Cotton	Vegetable Oils	Total Net Welfare Change
Benin	0.00	-3.86	-5.93	-0.80	-0.33	-0.20	-0.37	-0.14	0.03	-0.02	-11.60
Burkina Faso	0.00	0.05	-0.27	-0.06	0.01	0.08	0.18	-0.05	0.02	0.03	-0.02
Gambia	0.00	-0.29	-4.35	-0.61	-0.31	-0.01	-4.27	-0.31	0.00	-0.20	-10.35
Ghana	0.00	-0.97	-4.60	-3.51	-0.23	0.66	-2.19	2.84	0.00	-0.07	-8.07
Guinea	0.00	-0.08	-4.07	-2.30	-0.27	0.07	-2.95	-0.29	0.00	-0.12	-10.01
Guinea Bissau	0.00	-0.03	-0.21	-0.06	-0.01	0.00	-0.06	-0.01	0.00	-0.02	-0.38
Ivory Coast	0.15	-1.16	-7.32	-6.37	-0.15	2.86	-2.05	11.71	0.00	0.26	-2.07
Liberia	0.00	-0.28	-0.46	-0.38	-0.04	0.00	-0.15	-0.03	0.00	-0.03	-1.37
Mali	0.00	0.05	-5.59	-1.65	-0.07	0.00	-3.38	-1.33	0.00	-0.05	-12.09
Mauritania	0.00	-0.17	-2.71	-1.89	-0.06	-0.06	-2.74	-0.39	0.00	-0.13	-8.14
Niger	-0.04	0.02	-3.63	-0.33	0.05	-0.10	-0.80	-0.19	0.00	-0.09	-5.11
Nigeria	0.05	-0.07	-23.88	-24.46	-0.28	1.6	-21.54	-0.55	0.00	-0.85	-69.97
Senegal	0.00	-0.40	-10.26	-6.74	-0.04	-0.20	-2.08	-1.09	0.00	-0.24	-21.05
Sierra Leone	0.00	-0.17	-0.83	-0.49	-0.08	-0.03	-0.39	-0.11	0.00	-0.05	-2.15
Togo	0.00	-0.18	-3.12	-1.24	-0.16	-0.01	-0.73	-0.26	0.02	-0.11	-5.78
West Africa	0.16	-7.53	-77.23	-50.88	-1.96	4.63	-43.52	9.87	0.08	-1.69	-168.16
(B)											
Brazil	0.01	91.65	-19.25	-58.32	0.87	31.74	166.04	15.26	0.02	7.46	235.49
China	0.02	37.38	-13.65	4.08	10.96	30.92	-16.34	20.18	-0.05	1.09	74.58
India	0.04	18.43	17.45	44.94	-18.29	1.93	22.52	12.13	-0.14	-37.57	61.45
(C)											
EU	29.71	-6,269.14	-5,000.37	-3,244.45	66.67	580.88	-3,099.41	17,309.87	-0.22	7.51	381.06
Japan	13.16	298.56	-344.86	1,303.78	1,225.85	88.8	783.33	5,457.03	-0.08	1.06	8,826.64
USA	0.96	285.48	-2,263.51	-4.91	28.63	40.10	-649.29	-1,361.72	2.50	4.75	-3,917.02

Source: Authors' calculation from ATSPM simulation results.

$235.49 million) followed by China and India.[7] Such results contradict claims that developing countries will become worse off under WTO support system (Finger, 2008), but suggest that the large developing countries who are exporters of agricultural commodities will be better off from agricultural trade reforms, while the LDCs become worse off. Thus, unlike in West Africa, the large domestic market and better production technologies in the large developing countries coupled with their abilities to provide better production incentives for their producers (see Hansen et al., 2011), and export large surpluses afford them better opportunities of becoming the immediate beneficiaries of agricultural trade reform.

For the developed nations, the EU and Japan will be total net welfare gainers, while the United States becomes loser (see Table 5C). The EU's gains will largely be contributed by beverages, fruits, vegetables, livestock and vegetable oils, while its biggest losses will be encountered from trade in meat, dairy products and sugar. The biggest gains by Japan will be accumulated from beverages, grains, vegetables and sugar, while its major loss will be experienced from trade in dairy products. In the case of the United States, there are prospects for total welfare gains in trades in meat, fruits, vegetables, vegetable oils, cotton and livestock, but these gains are overwhelmed by the large losses encountered from the other commodities. Despite these minimum losses, export subsidies and domestic support reforms, nonetheless, turn out to be beneficial for the developed and large developing countries because most of them end up as gainers.

This result supports Anderson and Valenzuela's (2007) findings that removing agricultural trade distortion such as subsidies would increase farm income in both developed and developing countries. However, given the political sensitivity of agricultural policies in most of these developed countries (see Finger, 2008), the potential for welfare loss resulting from agricultural policy reform has made agricultural policy reform the most contentious at the Doha Round (see Anderson, 2009) and could hinder speedy conclusion of the negotiation. Such obstruction would be in the best interest of LDCs and net food importing countries to enable them make some radical adjustments in their domestic agricultural policies.

4. CONCLUDING REMARKS

In this paper, we analyse the potential welfare impacts West Africa tends to experience from reforming export subsidies and domestic support in developed and developing countries under the DDA. Our analysis is based on the July

---

[7] Brazil will experience total welfare loss in dairy products and grains; China experiences total losses in dairy products, sugar and cotton, and India experiences losses in vegetables, cotton and vegetable oils.

Framework scenario, which uses a tiered formula that adopts a Harbinson approach plus sensitive and SP. The findings reveal that, unlike the selected developed and large developing countries, all West African countries will become poorer as a result of export subsidies elimination and domestic support reduction. Nevertheless, except for livestock producers, producers of all other commodities analysed in the 15 countries considered within the region are potential winners. But the potential losses encountered by consumers of these commodities (except for livestock) cannot be compensated by producers' gains. Thus, all West African nations end up as net total welfare losers. These findings support those of other studies (e.g. Anderson and Martin, 2006; Peters, 2006), carried out on the effect of global agricultural trade reform on LDCs whose poverty reduction concern has been used by most development institutions and organisations as the basis for argument to ram agricultural trade reform. These results therefore leave us with the opinion that poor countries such as those in the region are not fully prepared for the implications of the agricultural trade reform proposal of the DDA.

That is, as agricultural trade reform contributes to global food price increases, consumers' purchasing power will fall while more foreign exchange will be needed by West African governments to import these major food commodities from the developed and net food exporting countries. With the dismal economic performance of the economies of most of the nations in the region along with the current economic down-turn, the implications will be more poverty and heightened food insecurity as all West African countries faced severe hunger situation in 2010 (see von Grebmer et al., 2010). The alarming level of food insecurity resulting from high food prices could further increase the political instability of the region as violent food protests occurred in five of the countries in the region between January 2007 and June 2008.[8] Thus, while some economists assume that the high food prices will encourage farmers readjust production to meet growing demand and make more profit in the long run, but in the long run, West African children would have died of starvation before the poor and incentive-deprived producers in the region can even readjust production to meet domestic demand.

Although the findings of this study conform to those of other previous works on the topic, concerns of data quality and reliability render these results more indicative than definitive. However, to avert some of the potentially negative effects of agricultural trade reforms, the region must first undertake agricultural transformation before aggressively pushing for reforms under the DDA. That is, regional leaders should raise agricultural budgetary allotment above the minimum 10 per cent budgetary allocation which the Maputo Declaration called on African

---

[8] Between January 1, 2007 and June 2008, violent food protests occurred in Niger, Burkina Faso, Guinea, Ivory Coast and Senegal.

governments to provide annually for agricultural development, and further inten-sify regional agricultural research.[9]

In addition, West African governments should focus on developing technologi-cal infrastructure and improving food self-sufficiency to reduce the dependency of the region on imports. Moreover, increasing supply-side factors such as strength-ening institutions and upgrading other relevant infrastructures for agricultural development and providing farmers better incentives to enable them access improved agricultural inputs and production technologies would be a reasonable priority for countries in the region. Also, given that most West African countries enjoy a competitive advantage in livestock production (indicative of the net welfare gains in livestock trade by most countries in the region), promotion of intra-African trade through regional integration would help reduce the excessive reliance on imported food from policy-active countries like the EU and United States. Finally, governments should take advantage of the Sino-Africa cooperation to explore the possibilities of transferring adaptable agricultural technologies already developed in China.

REFERENCES

Anderson, K. (2009), 'Distorted Agricultural Incentives and Economic Development: Asia's Experience', *The World Economy*, **32**, 3, 351–84.
Anderson, K. and W. Martin (2006), 'Agriculture, Trade Reform and the Doha Agenda', in K. Anderson and W. Martin (eds.), *Agricultural Trade Reform and the Doha Development Agenda* (Basingstoke, UK: Palgrave Macmillan; Washington, DC: World Bank), 3–36.
Anderson, K. and E. Valenzuela (2007), 'Do Global Trade Distortions Still Harm Developing Country Farmers?', *Review of World Economics*, **143**, 1, 108–39.
Anderson, K., W. Martin and D. van der Mensbrugghe (2006a), 'Market and Welfare Implications of Doha Reform Scenarios', in K. Anderson and W. Martin (eds.), *Agricultural Trade Reform and the Doha Development Agenda* (Basingstoke, UK: Palgrave Macmillan; Washington, DC: World Bank), 333–99.
Anderson, K., W. Martin and D. van der Mensbrugghe (2006b), 'Distortions to World Trade: Impacts on Agricultural Markets and Farm Incomes', *Review of Agricultural Economics*, **28**, 2, 168–94.
Baker, D. (2006), 'The WTO and the World's Poor', Available at: http://www.truthout.org/article/dean-baker-the-wto-and-worlds-poor (accessed 14 September 2009).
Binswanger-Mkhize, H. and A. McCalla (2008), 'The Changing Context and Prospect for Agricultural and Rural Development in Africa', *AfDB-IFAD Joint Evaluation of ARD in Africa*, Available at: http://www.ieri.org.za/documents/reports/Binswanger%20&%20McCalla_2008.pdf (accessed 15 March 2010).

---

[9] At a conference of the Ministers of Agriculture of the African Union held in Maputo, Mozambique 1–2 July 2003, African Ministers of Agriculture committed their countries to providing at least 10 per cent of their national budgetary resources for implementation of the Comprehensive Africa Agriculture Development Programme (CAADP). This decision was endorsed by African Heads of State at the 4th Summit of ACP Heads of State and Government meeting in Maputo on 23 and 24 June 23, 2004.

Diagne, A. (2008), 'Rice Sector Development in Africa: Opportunities and Challenges', *African-Japanese Plenary Workshop on Rice Production*, Available at: http://www.bibalex.org/CSSP/Presentations/Attachments/Diagne (accessed 13 January 2010).

Finger, J. M. (2008), 'Developing Countries in the WTO System: Applying Robert Hudec's Analysis to the Doha Round', *The World Economy*, **31**, 7, 887–904.

Frith, M. (2005), 'Bitter Harvest: How EU Sugar subsidies Devastate Africa', *Independent Service*, Available at: http://www.independent.co.uk/environment/bitter-harvest (accessed 29 May 2008).

von Grebmer, K., B. Nestorova, A. Quisumbing and R. Fertziger (2010), 'Global Hunger Index: The Challenge to Hunger: Focus on the Crisis of Child Undernutrition', Welthungerhilfe, International Food Policy Research Institute, Available at: http://www.irishaid.gov.ie/Uploads/ghi10.pdf (accessed 28 July 2011).

Hansen, J., F. Tuan and A. Somwaru (2011), 'Do China's Agricultural Policies Matter for World Commodity Markets?' *China Agricultural Economic Review*, **3**, 1, 6–25.

Hertel, T. W. and R. Keeney (2006), 'What Is at Stake: The Relative Importance of Import Barriers, Export Subsidies and Domestic Support', in K. Anderson and W. Martin (eds.), *Agricultural Trade Reform and the Doha Development Agenda* (Basingstoke, UK: Palgrave Macmillan; Washington, DC: World Bank), 37–61.

Hertel, T. W., R. Keeney, M. Ivanic and L. A. Winters (2007), 'Distributional Effects of WTO Agricultural Reforms in Rich and Poor Countries', *Economic Policy*, **22**, 50, 289–337.

Hertel, T. W., R. Keeney, M. Ivanic and L. A. Winters (2008), 'Why Isn't the Doha Development Agenda More Poverty Friendly?' GTAP Working Paper No. 37, Purdue University, Available at: http://docs.lib.purdue.edu/cgi/viewcontent.cgi (accessed 25 November 2011).

Hoekman, B. and P. Messerlin (2006), 'Removing the Exception of Agricultural Export Subsidies', in K. Anderson and W. Martin (eds.), *Agricultural Trade Reform and the Doha Development Agenda* (Basingstoke, UK: Palgrave Macmillan; Washington, DC: World Bank), 195–220.

Jensen, H. G. and H. Zobbe (2006), 'Consequences of Reducing Limits on Aggregate Measurement of Support', in K. Anderson and W. Martin (eds.), *Agricultural Trade Reform and the Doha Development Agenda* (Basingstoke, UK: Palgrave Macmillan; Washington, DC: World Bank), 245–70.

Kwiecinski, A. (2008), 'Do Agricultural Policies in China Support Farmers' Income?', in X. S. Zhang, X. Y. Li and P. Ho (eds.), *China's Agricultural Transition: Balancing Rural-Urban Relations* (Beijing: Social Science Academic Press), 157–68.

Murphy, S., B. Lilliston and M. B. Lake (2005), 'WTO Agreement on Agriculture: A Decade of Dumping', United States Dumping on Agricultural Markets IATP Publication No.1, A series assessing the World Trade Organization' first 10 years, 1995–2005; Available at: http://www.eldis.org/assets/Docs/16691.html (accessed 23 February 2010).

Nebehay, S. (2006), 'UN Food Envoy Slams Europe over Hunger Refugees', Available at: http://www.globalpolicy.org/component/content/article/217/46136.html (accessed 24 December 2008).

Oxfam (2004), 'Where's the Moral Fiber', *Oxfam International*, Available at: http://www.global-policy.org/component/content/article/220/47358.html (accessed 24 August 2009).

Panagariya, A. (2004), 'Subsidies and Trade Barriers: Alternative Perspective 10.2', in B. Lomborg (ed.), *Global Crises, Global Solutions* (New York: Cambridge University Press), 592–602.

Peters, R. (2006), 'Roadblock to Reform: The Persistence of Agricultural Export Subsidies', *Policy Issues in International Trade and Commodities Study Series* **32**, Available at: http://www.unctad.org/en/docs/itcdtab33_en.pdf (accessed 12 October 2009).

Schnepf, R. and J. Womach (2006), 'Potential Challenges to U.S. Farm Subsidies in the WTO', Available at: http://www.nationalaglawcenter.org (accessed 20 January 2010).

Schnepf, R. and J. Womach (2007), 'CRS Report for Congress: Potential Challenges to U.S. Farm Subsidies in the WTO', http://www.nationalaglawcenter.org (accessed 28 February 2009).

Summer, D. A. (2006), 'Reducing Cotton Subsidies: The DDA Cotton Initiative', in K. Anderson and W. Martin (eds.), *Agricultural Trade Reform and the Doha Development Agenda* (Basingstoke, UK: Palgrave Macmillan; Washington, DC: World Bank), 271–92.

Vanzetti, D. and B. Graham (2002), 'Simulating Agricultural Policy Reform with ATPSM', European Trade Study Group Annual Conference, Kiel, Available at: http://r0.unctad.org/ditc/tab/publications/Kiel.pdf (accessed 12 October 2009).

WTO (2003), 'Negotiations on Agriculture: First Draft for Modalities for further Commitments (Revision)', Available at: http://www.wto.org/english/tratop_e/agric_e/negoti_mod2stdraft_e.htm#marketacces (accessed 12 February 2009).

WTO (2007), Revised Draft Modalities for Agriculture, Available at: http://www.wto.org/english/tratop_e/agric_e/negoti_mod2stdraft_e.htm#marketacces (accessed 15 November 2009).

5

Taking Stock of Antidumping, Safeguards and Countervailing Duties, 1990–2009

Chad P. Bown

1. INTRODUCTION

*T*HE major economies of the world trading system undertook a variety of approaches to liberalise trade during 1985–2009. *Multilateral* negotiations resulted in the initiation and completion of one round (Uruguay Round, 1986–94) which transformed the GATT to the WTO, and WTO members subsequently initiated further liberalisation negotiations in 2001 under the (still ongoing) Doha Round. A number of countries liberalised by negotiating and/or expanding access to partners through major *preferential* trade agreement initiatives: examples include the Canada–US Free Trade Agreement (CUSFTA) that was signed in 1987 and then extended to include Mexico in 1994 to create NAFTA, and Argentina and Brazil negotiated with other South American countries to form Mercosur in 1991. The European Community expanded from 10 countries to 12 in 1986 to 15 in 1995 to 25 in 2004 to 27 members of the European Union by 2007, and it also formed a customs union with Turkey that went into effect in the mid-1990s. India

I thank Piyush Chandra, Meredith Crowley, Jeff Drope, Bob Feinberg, Bernard Hoekman, Hiau Looi Kee, Jesse Kreier, Nuno Limão, Rod Ludema, Anna Maria Mayda, Rachel McCulloch, Niall Meagher, Jorge Miranda, Çaglar Ozden, Tom Prusa, Raymond Robertson, Michele Ruta, Robert Staiger, Patricia Tovar, Maurizio Zanardi, two anonymous referees and seminar participants at the Stanford SITE Conference, USITC, and World Bank for helpful comments. Aksel Erbahar and Lauren Deason provided outstanding research assistance. I gratefully acknowledge funding for this project from the World Bank's Multi-Donor Trust Fund. Any opinions expressed in this paper are the author's and should not be attributed to the World Bank. All remaining errors are my own.

responded to its balance of payments crisis of 1991–92 by cutting its applied tariffs through a *unilateral* liberalisation. Finally, China underwent 15 years of *accession* negotiations to realise WTO membership in 2001, and this locked in a number of its major tariff reductions. Regardless of the trade liberalisation path undertaken, a common result is that many of these economies currently have historically low applied import tariffs in place.

While WTO economies pursued different liberalisation routes to reduce and sustain lower applied tariffs over these 25 years, a second theme common to this period is that many increasingly adopted 'contingent' or 'administered' import protection under policies such as antidumping, safeguards and countervailing duties – what I refer to jointly as temporary trade barrier (TTB) policies. The combined result of these two phenomena is a new framework for the international trading system: exporters are simultaneously subject to low (on average) applied import tariffs, but they also face the threat of frequently changing – i.e., newly imposed or removed – TTBs. Such an institutional framework ultimately poses many research questions on transmission mechanisms through which government access to and use of TTB policies are economically important.

This paper characterises the institutional framework by providing an empirically based set of facts on the cross-country use of TTB policies over 1990–2009, taking stock of newly available, product-level data organised into the World Bank's Temporary Trade Barriers Database (Bown, 2010a). I begin by using the data to address a number of basic questions. For which countries and in what episodes are such TTB policies revealed through their use as being quantitatively important?[1] How were these TTB policies used and not used during the global economic crisis of 2008–09? What is the exporter incidence of such imposed policies, and how has this changed over time?

I begin Section 2 by constructing two new measures of annual, product-level 'stocks' and 'flows' of imported products *subject to* these TTBs. These measures are defined to address some of the main shortcomings of previous research. First, prior research has not constructed comprehensive estimates for how much of a country's imports were subject to TTBs at any point in time. Examining the 'stock' of such trade barriers in place was previously difficult because of the lack of data on both the timing of policy removals and the details of which harmonised system (HS) import products that TTBs covered. As such, previous work focused almost exclusively on industry-defined data covering annual counts of the initiation of *new* investigations and the imposition of *newly imposed* barriers – more limited

---

[1] Such policies could be important despite nonuse (or under-utilisation) – for example, as an outside option or off-the-equilibrium path behaviour – if they help facilitate efficiency-enhancing outcomes. For example, access to such policies may serve as insurance for uncertain trade policy negotiators which allow them to take on deeper commitments in a trade agreement (Fischer and Prusa, 2003; Hoekman and Kostecki, 2009).

'flow' variables that also lacked economically satisfying definitions for a product. I overcome some of these difficulties by applying my measures to new and detailed data drawn from the World Bank's Temporary Trade Barriers Database. As such, this research builds upon prior work documenting the global proliferation of anti-dumping (AD) use in particular (Prusa, 2001; Zanardi, 2004; Bown, 2009).

My first estimates compare developed versus developing economy use of TTBs and show how such policies are likely to have heterogeneous economic impacts on these two types of economies' own trade flows.[2] Most striking is how the divergence between these two groups of policy-imposing economies has taken place over time. Even before the global economic shock of 2008–09, the annual stock of imported products subject to such trade barriers imposed by major emerging economies such as Argentina, Brazil, China, India and Turkey had grown substantially; from a starting point in the mid-to-late 1990s at or close to zero, to coverage of up to 4 per cent of each economy's imported products by 2007. On the other hand, more developed economies with a longer history of using such policies, like the United States and EU, have experienced a declining share of their imports subject to such policies over time. One of my measures indicates that while 3.5–5 per cent of these economies' imports may have been affected during 1997–2005, TTB policy coverage had fallen by roughly 50 per cent to only 1.5–3 per cent of their annual imports by 2007.[3]

After providing a broad characterisation of the use of these policies across countries over time, I use the methodological framework to assess the use of TTBs during the global economic shock of the 2008–09 crisis. Especially early in the crisis, and perhaps because of the sharp and unexpected decline in global trade flows in the fourth quarter 2008 through the first quarter 2009, there was substantial concern of a protectionist retreat on the scale of the 1930s Great

---

[2] These results relate to recent research (Vandenbussche and Zanardi, 2010; Egger and Nelson, forthcoming) that uses more historical, albeit less-detailed, data to estimate the aggregate impact of antidumping – the most common of these TTB policies – on trade flows. These two papers use similar gravity model regression approaches and present distinct results: while both find the effect of antidumping on trade flows to be negative, Egger and Nelson conclude that the effect is modest while Vandenbussche and Zanardi interpret the effect as more sizable. A separate approach to estimating the impact of these policies is Gallaway et al. (1999), which develop a computable general equilibrium-based approach to estimate the economic welfare impact of the US use of antidumping and countervailing duties on data for 1993.

[3] As I explain in substantial detail in the methodological section of the Appendix A, despite innovations that improve measurement of the economic importance of such TTBs, remaining data constraints leave some measurement error, especially when it comes to the construction of the *level* of any policy-imposing economy's imports subject to TTBs. Nevertheless, because I define the measures consistently over time and across trading partners, measurement error is much *less* of a concern for two of our main questions of interest: intertemporal changes (i.e. whether the scope of imported products subject to a country's use of TTBs is increasing or decreasing over time) and the relative exporter incidence (i.e. whether certain exporters are relatively more or less frequently targeted than others by imposed TTBs).

Depression era.[4] Nevertheless, in Section 3, I detail the somewhat surprising evidence that the 2008–09 shock basically continued precrisis trends in how both developed and developing economies apply new import protection via TTBs. While the major G20 users have combined to increase the stock of product lines subject to TTBs by 25 per cent during the crisis, and despite the massive recessions in many high-income economies, on average, the *developed* G20 economies increased the stock of products covered by TTBs by only 5 per cent in 2009 relative to the precrisis level.[5] On the other hand, developing economies have increased their stock of product coverage by TTBs during the crisis by 40 per cent, though there is substantial heterogeneity within the set of developing economies. Nevertheless, my results suggest it would be wrong to interpret this increase as *caused by* the crisis, given that the measured increase is consistent with precrisis trends and is not far from forecasts of what may have taken in place even in the absence of the crisis.[6]

The other major empirical exercise of the paper is to measure the exporter incidence of the growing use of antidumping so as to determine implications for discriminatory patterns of import protection across the trading system. The results are detailed in Section 4; not surprisingly, there is also evidence of substantial heterogeneity of impact across affected exporting economies. Over time, the main impact of the foreign use of antidumping is increasingly on developing economy exporters. First, China's exported products face the largest stocks of foreign-imposed antidumping barriers by 2009, at nearly four times the amount of the next most targeted economies – South Korea; EU; and Taiwan, China. Overall, by 2009, 2.6 per cent of China's exported products to developing economies were subject to antidumping, and 1.6 per cent of its products to developed economies were subject to antidumping, percentages that had accelerated since its 2001 WTO

---

[4] For a comprehensive account and decomposition of the various protectionist forces at work during the Great Depression, as well as other, nontrade policy-related factors that contributed to the curtailment of global trade, see Irwin (2011). For an early assessment of potential causes of the trade collapse of 2008–09, of which the consensus is that it had little to do with changes in trade policy but instead more fundamental demand (income) and supply (credit) factors, see Baldwin (2009). Baldwin and Evenett (2009) provide a collection of research from early in the crisis that highlights the fears of an impending protectionist backlash.

[5] Russia (not a WTO member) and Saudi Arabia (previously not a TTB user) are the only G20 economies not represented in the empirical analysis of the use of TTBs.

[6] It is not too early to begin to assess the stock of products subject to TTBs resulting from the crisis period given that increased flows of new investigations had shown signs of levelling off by the end of 2009. Furthermore, my measurement of TTBs 'times' the contribution to the stock of newly imposed TTBs as the year the first (even a preliminary) barrier is imposed. While terminating coverage for policies imposed as of the end of 2009 is likely to miss some late-imposed barriers, as of the July 2010 Temporary Trade Barriers Database release (covering data through second quarter (2Q) 2010), there had been a substantial moderation in the count of newly initiated TTB investigations relative to the run-up that took place in 2008–09. The count of new investigations began to taper off in 4Q 2009, and this has continued into 1Q and 2Q 2010. For a discussion, see, for example, Bown (2010b).

accession (Messerlin, 2004; Bown, 2010c). I illustrate additional data that show how this 'South–South' feature of antidumping is also not unique to China's exports. A number of other developing countries face trends similar to China in that the share of their products exported to other emerging economies that is targeted by foreign antidumping is higher than the share of their products exported to high-income economies.

In addition to these two main empirical contributions, I use my approach to address a number of other research questions. For example, while focusing on annual stock measures of TTBs is an important and previously underemphasised area for research, my methodology also allows for construction of other measures of TTB policy activity, including more precise 'flow' measures based on product coverage. Capturing more information on the rate of new application of such barriers over time illustrates the volatility of trade policy and raises additional questions regarding policy uncertainty that have emerged elsewhere in the literature (e.g. Limão and Handley, 2010). While there is substantial variation in flows both across countries and over time, in Section 2, I also find that some major economies average up to 1 per cent of imported products becoming subject to new TTB investigations annually. Furthermore, there is also evidence that the flows relate to the *cumulative* stocks of 6-digit HS products affected by at least one TTB over 1990–2009. My examination of the data suggests that for the major G20 economies, the cumulative stock of affected products ranges from a low of 0.09 per cent (Japan) to a high of 21.79 per cent (Mexico), with India (8.62 per cent), European Union (9.62 per cent) and United States (13.37 per cent) in the middle. The uncertainty created by the volatility in some economies' use of TTBs is a policy feature quite distinct from how most of these economies use their applied tariffs, at least during the 2000s, which have remained relatively unchanged given their multilateral (WTO) and preferential trade agreement commitments.

Next, I also investigate the potential for substitutability across antidumping, countervailing duty (CVD) and safeguard barriers within these policy-using economies; as such, I attempt to disentangle the relative importance of each policy across countries and time.[7] For example, in addition to the global safeguard (SG), I include data on post-2001 use of the 'China-safeguard' (CSG) – a policy that the existing WTO membership insisted upon as part of China's accession to the WTO and that may be imposed until 2014.[8] The most prominent use of this policy was the high-profile US-imposed safeguard on imports of Chinese tires in the midst of the global crisis in September 2009. Overall, evidence from Section 2

---

[7] Examples of recent research examining use and other impacts of antidumping across (including developing) countries include Niels and Francois (2006), Bown (2008), Reynolds (2009), Moore and Zanardi (2009) and Bown and Tovar (2011).

[8] Bown and Crowley (2010) examine whether there is empirical evidence that might motivate inclusion of a 'trade deflection' provision in the terms triggering use of the CSG under its 2001 WTO accession agreement.

allows me to conclude that while antidumping is still the dominant TTB policy instrument, an exclusive focus on antidumping could miss up to 40 per cent (depending on policy-imposing economy) of the cumulative stock of products affected by TTBs during this period; though most of this is with respect to the *global* safeguard policy instrument.

Third, in Section 5, I provide a final examination of the more recent potential shift towards governments relying on the countervailing duty (anti-subsidy) policy. Such a change in the policymaking environment stems from at least two separate events: the rules and commitments accompanying China's WTO accession in the face of its continued export expansion; and the global policy response to the economic crisis of 2008–09 which led to a number of government-financed industry bailouts which trading partners may ultimately choose to address through CVDs. I decompose the data and illustrate that CVD use is still largely dominated by the United States, though I point out signs identifying how this may change over time. I also illustrate how assessing the impact of CVDs is complicated by the fact that almost all applications in recent history have been made simultaneously with antidumping duties (against the same products, from the same foreign sources). The evolving nature of antidumping, countervailing duty and safeguard protection has obvious political economy implications for which countries are interested in negotiating potential reform to the WTO Agreement on Antidumping, Agreement on Subsidies and Countervailing Measures and Agreement on Safeguards.

I conclude the final section by using the facts that the data reveal to raise new and pressing questions for further economic research on TTB use and the evolving rules, changing nature of the WTO membership, shifting global trade patterns, interaction with preferential trade arrangements and even the fragmentation of global production.

2. THE STOCK OF TEMPORARY TRADE BARRIERS – FROM THE IMPORTING ECONOMY PERSPECTIVE

My first task is to construct measures for the use and potential impact of the TTBs over time and across policy-using countries. My attempt is to improve upon earlier efforts (Prusa, 2001; Zanardi, 2004; Bown, 2009) to characterise the use of such trade barriers across countries over time. Previous work generally suffers from two data-induced shortcomings. First, it typically relies on the country's own, self-reported characterisation of a 'product' subject to a newly initiated investigation or imposed barrier, and this definition of a product results from the petition filed by the domestic industry. There is no uniform standard for such definitions, as such using this unit of account may not accurately reflect the economic importance or unimportance of TTBs if there is substantial heterogeneity in the amount of product coverage across TTB investigations, countries or time. Second, previous work also focused almost exclusively on data covering annual counts of the initiation of *new* investigations and the imposition of *newly imposed* barriers – i.e., 'flow' variables. Such research has typically not had access to sufficiently informative data so as to construct and examine the 'stock' build-up of such trade barriers in place over time because it lacked information on policy removals.[9] Constructing and examining stock measures also allows me to better assess the incidence of TTBs in the face of heterogeneity in the timing of newly imposed barriers and the length of time that such barriers stay imposed.

While I leave to the Appendix A an equation-based description of my explicit methodology, here, I provide a brief discussion to lend intuition to the approach.

My first methodological approach constructs 'count' measures of the annual stock of HS-06 products subject to TTBs, and it takes an importing economy's set of HS-06 products as the unit of observation. I build from Bown and Tovar (2011, Figure 1) which focused on India's use of antidumping over 1992–2003; the count measures reflect information on newly imposed trade barriers, previously imposed trade barriers and the removal of previously imposed barriers. In addition to applying the Bown and Tovar approach to a new set of countries, I also adapt it along three important dimensions: (i) I examine not only cumulative stocks but also flows; (ii) I examine not only antidumping, but also HS-06 products subject to other TTB policies such as CVDs, global safeguards and China-specific safeguards; and (iii) I normalise the count of affected HS-06 products by the economy's stock of HS-06 products with nonzero imports in that year.

My second approach refines the counts measure by using import value data to *trade-weight* the importance of TTBs at the HS-06 product level. Creation of this complementary 'value' measure is one way to address the likelihood of substantial heterogeneity in the economic importance across HS-06 products and TTBs. For example, not all HS-06 products may be equally important contributors to the economy's overall level of imports; one product from one foreign source may cover billions of dollars of imports while another may only cover a few hundred thousand dollars. Furthermore, some TTBs are applied against multiple foreign sources and thus have the possibility of adversely affecting much more trade than one applied against a single foreign supplier of the HS-06 product. The values approach requires HS-06 import value data from the United Nations Comtrade database to construct year-by-year coverage ratios of imports subject to TTBs. I use nonoil imports only.

The Appendix provides an explicit account of the methodology for the 'count' and 'value' computations, as well as a more complete discussion of additional caveats. My empirical analysis relies on the extremely detailed TTB policy data from the World Bank's Temporary Trade Barriers Database (Bown, 2010a) to

---

[9] Exceptions include recent research examining the question of antidumping policy removal and the Sunset Review process such as Moore (2006) and Cadot et al. (2007).

FIGURE 1
Developed (G20) Economy Use of Temporary Trade Barriers, 1990–2009.

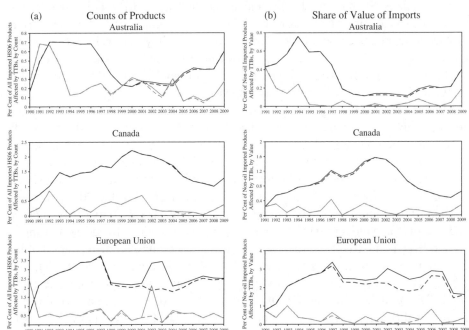

construct relatively comprehensive information on the 'stock' and 'flow' of such barriers at the 6-digit HS product level across countries and over time. More details on the data are available in Appendix B and are described comprehensively in Bown (2010a).

a. Potential Trade Impact From the Importing Economy Perspective

Before turning to the results, I describe how to interpret the data presented in Figures 1 and 2. Each row presents information for one policy-imposing economy. The panels in the left column (Figures 1a and 2a) present information based on the 'count' of HS-06 products and thus minimal assumptions tying product coverage to trade impacts. The panels in the right column (Figures 1b and 2b) rely on a trade-weighted measure of time-varying coverage ratios by matching HS-06 products to import 'value' data. The series in panel a begins in 1990. The series in panel b covers TTB activity beginning in 1991, since the 'value' approach requires import value data for $t - 1$, and my first year of available import data for most economies is only 1990.[10]

---

[10] See Appendix equation (A1) (for 'count' approach) and equation (A2) (for 'value' approach). There are exceptions for countries for which HS-06 import data are not available back until 1990; these countries are listed in the Appendix B.

FIGURE 1 *Continued*

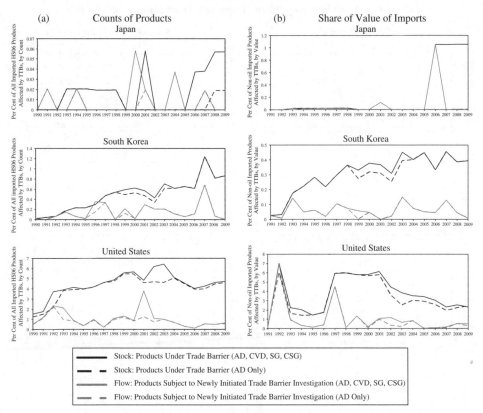

Source: Calculated using Appendix equation (A1) (panel a) and equation (A2) (panel b) from data in the Temporary Trade Barriers Database (Bown, 2010a).

Each of the panels in Figures 1 and 2 presents four different pieces of information. First, the *grey solid* line defines the TTB indicator based on imported products affected by newly initiated *investigations* under *any* TTB policy and thus is a broad measure of the potential annual 'flow' of new barriers.[11] Second, the *grey dashed* line defines the indicator similarly, but it captures the flow of potential imported products affected by the *antidumping* policy alone. For countries that only used antidumping and did not have any CVD, SG or CSG investigations during this

---

[11] This series represents the *potential* new product coverage because not all resulting investigations necessarily result in the imposition of a new trade barrier. I use this definition given the results of Staiger and Wolak (1994) which noted how even the mere investigation can have real economic effects. Thus, the 'flow' level can be higher than the incremental addition to the 'stock' given that not all investigations will result in imposed barriers. For an example of this, see the 'count' measures for Brazil in Figure 2a and the years 1993 (investigations = 'flow') and 1994 (new barriers = 'stock' imposed one year later).

FIGURE 2
Developing (G20) Economy Use of Temporary Trade Barriers, 1990–2009

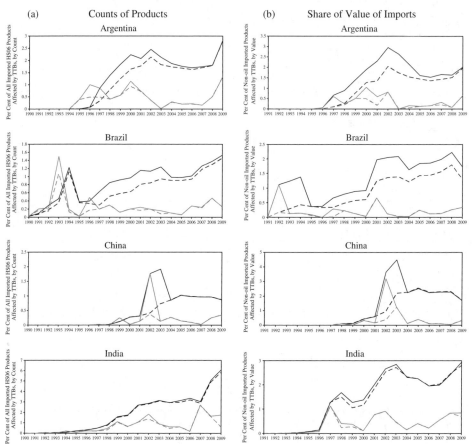

period, the grey solid line and the grey dashed line overlap. Any divergence between these two lines represents the products subject to investigations under the countries' other (nonantidumping) TTB policies. Third, the *black solid* line defines the TTB indicator as taking on a value of 1 whenever the product (panel a) or product-trading partner combination (panel b) was subject to some TTB that had been imposed in that year or a prior year (and had not yet been removed); as such this measures the 'stock' of products subject to TTBs. Fourth, the *black dashed* line represents the stock of products subject to antidumping policy only.

(i) Developed Economy Imposers of TTBs

Begin with Figure 1, which illustrates the results for the main developed G20-economy users of TTBs. Consider the case of a policy-imposing country like the

FIGURE 2 *Continued*

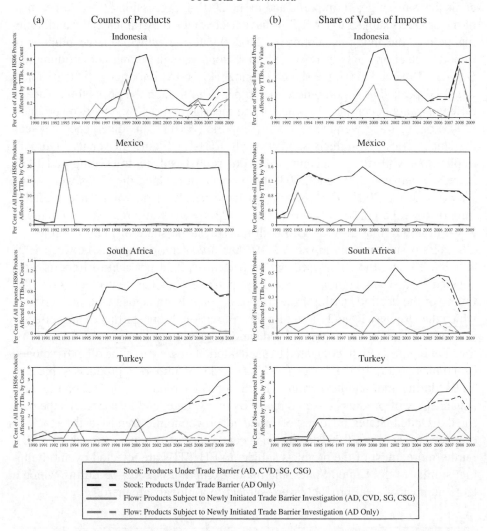

Source: Calculated using Appendix equation (A1) (panel a) and equation (A2) (panel b) from data in the Temporary Trade Barriers Database (Bown, 2010a).

United States.[12] The consistency of the data on the use of TTBs with broad macroeconomic trends is visible in both Figure 1a, b; spikes in flows (and increases

---

[12] The United States had been using these policies (antidumping in particular) prior to 1990. Since I am starting with barriers first imposed in 1990, there is an underlying stock of products affected by these policies that I am not capturing. (This is because of consistency of access to import classification under the HS which took hold across countries only in 1988.) This will also apply to Australia, Canada and the European Union who each had a substantial stock of antidumping barriers in place by the time the HS system started in 1988.

to stocks) take place in the 1990–91 recession, in response to the 1997–98 Asian crisis that saw surges in imports, and in the 2001–02 recession.[13] Over time, most of the products subject to a US TTB have been affected by (at least) the antidumping policy; the major exception is 2002–03 during which a large number of imported steel products were subject to a global safeguard and not antidumping. Between 1997 and 2007, the share of annual HS-06 US imported products subject to a TTB peaked at slightly more than 6 per cent, though the peaks took place in different years depending on whether the measurement is by *counts* of products (2003) or the trade-weighted *value* of imports (2001). This divergence between the stock series of products subject to all TTBs in Figure 1a versus Figure 1b implies that while the (net) count of HS-06 products subject to US-imposed TTBs increased between 2001 and 2003, the products for which the TTBs were being *removed* during 2001–03 were a much larger share of the value of overall US imports than the products for which new TTBs were being imposed.[14] Finally, it is worth noting that according to both measures, the share of imports subject to US TTBs is substantially lower in 2007 than it was during its peak between 1997 and 2007. Using the *value* approach in particular, 2.33 per cent of imports were covered in 2007 as compared to a 2001 peak of 6.14 per cent of imports. The timing of the decline starting from that peak roughly coincides with the period at which the Uruguay Round Sunset Review provisions were starting to take effect.[15]

Consider next some of the other developed economy imposers of TTBs illustrated in Figure 1. First, compared to the United States, each of the other developed economies generally has lower *levels* of stocks of imported products subject to TTBs during the sample period. The European Union has the second-highest annual stock of products covered by TTBs on average, and its use tracks the data for the United States in terms of broad macroeconomic trends in the stock of product coverage, and the decline in recent years of products subject to TTBs. Furthermore, most of the products subject to EU TTBs are affected by antidumping; similar to the United States, the major exception is 2002–03 during which a large number of steel products were subject to a global safeguard.

---

[13] This is consistent with other research linking antidumping use, in particular, with business cycle fluctuations such as changes in real GDP and currency movements. See Knetter and Prusa (2003).

[14] The share of imports for products that had been subject to a previous TTB that was being removed would be based on what the product's share of the US import market had been *prior* to the TTB first being imposed. See again the discussion of Appendix equation (A2).

[15] Under Article 18.3.2 of the Uruguay Round's Antidumping Agreement, for sunset purposes, an AD barrier imposed prior to 1995 was deemed to have been imposed on the date of entry into force of the Antidumping Agreement (1 January 1995). Thus, by the end of 1999, the United States had to initiate sunset reviews on all barriers imposed prior to 1995 that were still in effect in 1999. Presumably, a number of these reviews were completed during 2000–02, and when combined with the normal removal of barriers imposed after 1995, this led to sharper reductions in the 'stock' of products subject to antidumping in particular (especially using the 'value' measure) after 2000–02.

TABLE 1
G20 Economies' Annual Stock of Imports subject to TTBs, 1997–2009

G20 Economy Imposer (Ranked by Column 3)	2009			1997–2007			
	Count of HS-06 Products Subject to TTB (1)	Import Share, by Count (2)	Import Share, by Value (3)	Average Annual Import Share, by Count (4)	Average Annual Import Share, by Value (5)	Minimum Annual Import Share, by Value (6)	Maximum Annual Import Share, by Value (7)
Developing economies							
Turkey	273	5.31	3.05	1.92	2.02	1.32	3.35
India	308	6.09	2.94	2.34	1.97	1.27	2.85
Argentina	139	2.81	2.01	1.82	1.79	0.67	2.96
Brazil	78	1.53	1.73	1.01	1.52	0.66	2.09
China	46	0.87	1.71	0.75	1.70	0.00	4.49
Mexico	58	1.09	0.68	19.91	1.15	0.93	1.59
Indonesia	24	0.49	0.68	0.38	0.35	0.12	0.75
South Africa	40	0.76	0.25	0.96	0.42	0.32	0.54
High-income economies							
United States	256	4.72	2.33	5.11	4.58	2.33	6.14
European Union	137	2.50	1.59	2.62	2.69	2.38	3.37
Japan	3	0.06	1.06	0.02	0.21	0.00	1.05
Canada	69	1.27	0.64	1.71	1.10	0.52	1.57
Australia	31	0.60	0.40	0.32	0.18	0.11	0.45
South Korea	39	0.86	0.39	0.64	0.38	0.30	0.46

Notes:
(i) TTB = temporary trade barrier.
(ii) Columns (2) and (4) are computed using equation (A1) and columns (3), (5), (6) and (7) use equation (A2).
Source: compiled by the author from the Temporary Trade Barriers Database (Bown, 2010a), imports data from Comtrade.

With respect to the other major developed economies, historical users of anti-dumping such as Australia and Canada have also experienced a downward trend in the share of their imported products subject to TTBs during this period, with the exception of 2008–09. South Korea is a relatively new user, though the stock of imported products subject to its TTBs has increased moderately over time. The least active TTB user amongst the set of G20 developed economies during this period is Japan. Japan had an extremely small number of its imported products (panel a) subject to TTBs; nevertheless, when tradeweighting at the HS-06 level, as in panel b, the 2006 imposition of CVDs against imported semiconductors from South Korea has covered a significantly larger fraction of imports.

The lower half of Table 1 summarises the stock information across the economies illustrated in Figure 1. The economies are ordered according to their *value* share measure of imports covered by the stock of TTBs in effect in 2009 (column 3). The table also reports data on the raw count of HS-06 products subject to TTBs in 2009, the *count* share measure for 2009, the annual average for 1997–2007 of affected imports, and the minimum and maximum *value* share measures during that period.[16]

(ii) Developing Economy Imposers of TTBs

Figure 2 presents information in the same form as Figure 1 but with respect to the G20 *developing* countries. The broad pattern of developing economy-imposed TTBs over this time period is much different from the developed economy users.

Consider first a major emerging market like India. In response to its balance of payments crisis of 1991–92, India entered a stand-by arrangement with the IMF in which one of the conditions was a substantial unilateral reduction of its applied import tariffs over 1992–97. According to widely-used measures that rely on counts of the number of newly initiated investigations or imposed barriers (thus without normalising for product coverage or the economic importance of imports), India has become the WTO system's most frequent user of policies like antidumping and the global safeguard. India first started using antidumping in 1992, but by 1997, it began to accumulate sizable stocks of products under TTBs (primarily antidumping) according to my two measures illustrated in Figure 2a, b. The stock of affected products continued to increase through the 2000s, and by 2009, India had a stock of TTBs in place that covered 6.09 per cent (2.94 per cent) of its imports according to the count (value) measure. And while India is now a user of each of the four TTB policy instruments – it has filed the most antidumping, global safeguard and China-specific safeguard investigations during this period, and it filed its first CVD investigation in 2009 – Figure 2 also illustrates that antidumping has been the instrument that has affected the majority of products impacted by India's total use of TTBs.

Other emerging economies such as Argentina, Brazil and Turkey have similar patterns to their data on TTB product coverage over time. For Argentina and Brazil, there is a general upward trend in the stock of imported products subject to TTBs after they undertook preferential (reciprocal) trade liberalisation embodied in the Mercosur agreement in the early 1990s. There are also upward spikes in flows (and stock accumulations) around 2000 that correspond to the Argentine financial crisis and currency devaluation. For these two countries, there is also evidence of economically sizable use of nonantidumping TTBs during the 1990s, most of which is the result of the global safeguard. Like Argentina and Brazil,

---

[16] To interpret the magnitude of the count of HS-06 products, note that there are slightly more than 5,000 HS-06 product categories in existence in any one year in the sample. While most of the developed economies and many of the developing economies had nonzero imports of close to 100 per cent of all products in all years, this is not universally the case. India, for example, began the 1990s by importing only around 68 per cent of all HS-06 product categories. By 2001, that share had increased to 90 per cent.

Turkey experienced a similar increase in the stock of its products covered by TTBs after its formation and phasing in of a customs union (with the European Union) after 1995, as well as implementation of its Uruguay Round WTO commitments. Both of these actions constrained Turkey's ability to unilaterally change its applied import tariffs and may have shifted any political pressure to impose new trade barriers onto previously unused TTB policy instruments.

China began using TTBs with its first antidumping case in 1997. Figure 2 indicates a steady, but moderate increase in products covered by its use of AD beginning shortly thereafter. The break in the trend for China is 2002–03 when it, like the EU, followed the US lead and imposed a global safeguard over a large number of imported steel products. The result was a spike to 4.49 per cent of the stock of imports (by value) covered by TTBs in 2003. The tradeweighting in this case reflects a larger economic importance of these products in China's overall imports than the count measure, which was 1.92 per cent of all imported products in 2003.

Finally, consider the case of Mexico in Figure 2. Mexico imposed antidumping barriers on imports from China covering more than 1000 HS-06 products (more than 21 per cent of Mexico's imported products, see Figure 2a) in 1993 at duties that reached as high as 533 per cent, and these TTBs remained in place until they were finally removed in October 2008. However, because Mexico imposed such barriers *prophylactically* – i.e., 700 different HS-06 products with AD imposed in 1993 had *zero* imports from China in 1992 – cumulatively, the 1000 HS-06 product imports from China covered less than 0.8 per cent of Mexico's imports in 1992 (Figure 2b). Despite Mexico's AD being imposed on what would become some of China's major export product lines to the *world* by the late 1990s (e.g. textiles, clothing, footwear, toys, bicycles, electronics and chemicals), in this instance, the approach of trade-weighting the 1993 TTBs with 1992 import data tends to underemphasise the amount of Mexican trade likely to be affected over time (Figure 2b) relative to the *counts* approach.[17]

As such, the Mexican example is excellent motivation for my choice to report both the *count* measure and the *value* measure, as they complement each other and thus can provide a more complete and accurate assessment of the economic importance of an economy's TTB use. As the Mexican case reveals, the count measure may be particularly important in my context of studying many developing economy users of TTBs, some of which may follow a strategy similar to Mexico and implement the TTBs prophylactically and before the arrival of substantial imports of particular Chinese products. This is a possibility given that that each

---

[17] Mexico's use of antidumping against China in this instance was likely in anticipation of China's ultimate accession to the WTO (negotiations that began under the GATT in 1987) for which China's exporters would ultimately receive most-favoured nation treatment under Mexico's tariff schedule; see also de la Torre and Gonzalez (2005).

of the policy-imposing economies that I analyse heavily target imports from China, as I confirm in the data discussed in Section 4 below.

Finally, note again that the top half of Table 1 summarises the data on the developing economy users of TTBs presented in Figure 2.

b. Policy Volatility and Uncertainty

Thus far, my discussion of Figures 1 and 2 has focused primarily on each policy-imposing economy's 'stock' measures of annual products subject to TTBs. Nevertheless, each of the figures also presents information on the annual 'flow' of all TTBs (*grey solid* line) and antidumping alone (*grey dashed* line), as defined annually by products subject to newly initiated investigations. Table 2 summarises the 'flow' information from Figures 1 and 2 for each of these economies.

Table 2, column (1), documents (and orders policy-imposing economies by) the cumulative share of all HS-06 import products that the economy subjected to at least one TTB investigation over 1990–2009. The first country on the list is Mexico at 21.79 per cent, which is not surprising given my discussion of Mexico's antidumping against imports from China covering 1993–2008 (Figure 2a). Also not surprising for Mexico are columns (5) and (6), which show the annual average flow of products subject to new investigations during 1997–2007 as close to zero. There was little underlying demand in the Mexican economy for more TTBs each year given that such a large share of Mexico's imported products were already subject to a TTB during the entire period. On the other hand, consider an economy like India (8.62 per cent) with a smaller (although still sizable) cumulative share of total imported products that it had subjected to at least one TTB over the period. India had an average of 0.94 (0.50) per cent of imported products by count (value) being subject to new TTB investigations each year during 1997–2007. Its flow measure was much higher than Mexico because India built up its stock more slowly. India is not alone as other economies like the United States, EU, Turkey and Argentina each had flow measures that (by count) averaged more than 0.40 per cent of imported products per year during 1997–2007.

Combined, these results suggest that a number of major economies in the WTO system may create substantial trade policy uncertainty for foreign exporters through the way they use TTBs. While applied tariffs are quite low in this period, many exporters experienced the possibility of a trade policy adjustment by being subject to a TTB investigation which had a reasonable chance of resulting in imposition of a new trade barrier.

Finally, consider the Table 2 data that examine flow information on potential new TTBs during the recent global economic crisis. Columns (3) and (4) present information from 2009 on the investigations initiated in response to domestic industry petitions for new import protection. In 2009, 0.63 per cent (0.50 per cent) of US imports by count (value) were subject to a new TTB investigation. These

TABLE 2

Cumulative TTB Policy Coverage Over Time and Policy Volatility, 1990–2009

G20 Economy Imposer (Ranked by Column 1)	1990–2009		2009		1997–2007			
	Cumulative Share of Imported Products Ever Subject to a TTB, by Count (1)	Share of TTB-Subjected Products Affected by AD, by Count (2)	Annual Flow of Import Share, by Count (3)	Annual Flow of Import Share, by Value (4)	Average Annual Flow of Import Share, by Count (5)	Average Annual Flow of Import Share, by Value (6)	Minimum Annual Flow of Import Share, by Value (7)	Maximum Annual Flow of Import Share, by Value (8)
Developing economies								
Mexico	21.79	100.00	0.06	0.00	0.20	0.07	0.00	0.44
India	8.62	89.42	1.74	0.85	0.94	0.50	0.11	1.13
Turkey	6.63	71.95	0.80	0.09	0.43	0.21	0.00	0.92
Argentina	4.94	90.59	1.32	0.65	0.45	0.42	0.00	1.05
Brazil	3.80	80.09	0.26	0.34	0.19	0.18	0.02	0.66
China	2.74	59.75	0.34	0.32	0.26	0.52	0.00	3.21
South Africa	2.34	100.00	0.04	0.01	0.16	0.06	0.00	0.13
Indonesia	1.31	77.63	0.27	0.09	0.13	0.09	0.00	0.36
High-income economies								
United States	13.37	84.94	0.63	0.50	1.01	0.92	0.02	4.53
European Union	9.62	87.30	0.33	0.33	0.63	0.37	0.04	0.81
Canada	3.70	98.60	0.37	0.28	0.29	0.15	0.01	0.43
Australia	3.24	98.40	0.27	0.19	0.19	0.02	0.00	0.08
South Korea	2.44	89.44	0.00	0.01	0.20	0.07	0.00	0.15
Japan	0.09	0.00	0.00	0.02	0.01	0.11	0.00	1.05

Notes:
(i) TTB = temporary trade barrier.
(ii) Columns (1), (2), (3) and (5) are computed using Appendix equation (A1) and columns (4), (6), (7) and (8) use equation (A2).

Source: compiled by the author from the Temporary Trade Barriers Database (Bown, 2010a), imports data from *Comtrade*.

data are somewhat surprising given the historical context; at the time, there was a substantial fear that new import protection would result from the deep recession. Injured industries and high levels of unemployment could result in firms and labour unions placing demands for new barriers. However, the US figures for 2009 are well below the average annual share of imported products subject to new US TTB investigations during 1997–2007, which is 1.01 per cent (0.92 per cent) by count (value). This pattern is similar for the EU, South Korea, Japan and South Africa – economies that all registered smaller flow measures (new investigations) in 2009 than their 1997–2007 annual (precrisis) averages. On the other hand, India (1.74 per cent of imports, by count), Argentina (1.32 per cent) and Turkey (0.80 per cent) are countries with the opposite result; each had substantially higher 2009 flows than their 1997–2007 averages. I describe these and other notable 2008–09 crisis trends in the data in more detail in Section 3.

c. Policy Coverage and Focus on Antidumping

Before turning to a more detailed discussion of the 2008–09 crisis, I point to one last feature of Table 2. Column (2) presents information on the extent to which each of the G20 economies was particularly reliant on antidumping, relative to its total cumulation of products that were affected by at least one TTB during 1990–2009.

For economies like Mexico, South Africa, Australia and Canada, antidumping alone covered more than 98 per cent of the products that they subjected to a TTB during this period. And while some countries may use multiple policies simultaneously – e.g. antidumping and a CVD against the same product from the same foreign export source at the same time, an issue to which I return to in Section 5 below – this affects the size of the trade barrier imposed (e.g. the height of the new tariff), not the scope of import product coverage affected by TTBs.

On the other hand, there are some economies for which a singular focus on antidumping misses much of the product coverage associated with TTB use during 1990–2009. Both the United States and EU, for example, had more than 10 per cent of the products subject to some TTB policy during this period that was not antidumping. For China, it was over 40 per cent of all TTB-affected products. For these three economies, I have already discussed the main cause of this in the context of Figures 1 and 2; i.e., 2002–03 when these economies imposed global safeguards on a number of imported steel products. Nevertheless, other economies like Argentina, Brazil, Indonesia and Turkey that were not part of the 2002–03 steel safeguard-imposing group also have sizable shares (10–30 per cent) of TTB-affected products impacted from some policy *other than* antidumping. Despite India being the most frequent user of antidumping, because it is also a frequent user of safeguards and the China-specific safeguard, over 10 per cent of its TTB-affected products were impacted by some policy other than antidumping.

3. THE GLOBAL ECONOMIC CRISIS OF 2008–09

The global recession of 2008–09 served as a 'stress test' to the institutional structure of the multilateral trading system. Previous to the crisis, countries had lowered their applied tariffs but established a set of provisions under the WTO which granted themselves policy flexibility through resort to TTBs in the case of unforeseen events. An evolving consensus is that the response of the WTO system was positive; WTO members withstood the severe storm of uncertainty and economic trauma of the global crisis at least in the short term. Despite domestic economies going into recession, injured domestic industries, high rates of unemployment and political pressure for new import protection, there was not a major retreat towards raising applied tariffs, especially in ways that countries might have adopted in violation of their WTO commitments (Kee et al., 2010). Nevertheless, to the extent that these economies did respond with new policy initiatives, they turned to either the TTB policies that are my focus, to stimulus packages and bailouts (issues to which I return to in Section 5), or to some other nontariff barriers.

The last section began to describe some of the TTB policymaking during the crisis, illustrating heterogeneity across which countries experienced higher flows of imported products subject to new TTB investigations. One question is whether the countries with small flows also had relatively high *precrisis* stocks of products covered by previously imposed TTBs. For a number of the major developed economies in Figure 1, I can quickly rule out this explanation. Their precrisis trends had resulted in relatively low shares of imported products subject to the stock of TTBs in place prior to the crisis in 2007.

Consider Figure 3, which illustrates the data cumulated across G20 policy-imposing economies on the *combined* stocks of imported products subject to TTBs over 1997–2009, using the *count* method of measurement.[18] Figure 3a illustrates that, by the end of 2009, the G20 economies had increased the stock of imported products they subjected to imposed TTBs by 25.42 per cent relative to precrisis levels of 2007 (*black solid* line). By 2009, 2.15 per cent of HS-06 products that the G20 economies imported were now subject to a TTB, having increased from 1.88 per cent of imported products prior to the crisis in 2007. And for all the media attention focused on other policies, such as the China-specific transitional

---

[18] For reasons described above, Mexico is the only major G20 user of such policies not included in Figure 3 (see again Figure 2a).

CHAD P. BOWN

FIGURE 3
Combined G20* Use of Temporary Trade Barriers, 1997–2009

(a) Stock and Flow for Aggregate G20, All TTBs Versus AD Only

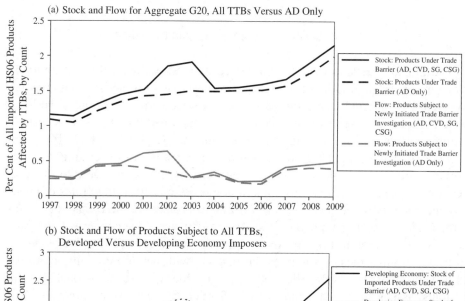

(b) Stock and Flow of Products Subject to All TTBs,
Developed Versus Developing Economy Imposers

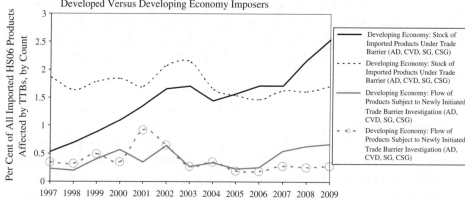

Notes:
The data are aggregated over the following thirteen G20 policy-imposing economies: Argentina, Australia, Brazil, Canada, China, the European Union, India, Indonesia, Japan, South Africa, South Korea, Turkey and the United States. Mexico is the only major G20 user of such policies not included in construction of the data for the figures, for reasons explained in the text (see also Figure 2).

Source: Calculated using a modified version of Appendix equation (A1) from data in the Temporary Trade Barriers Database (Bown, 2010a).

safeguard (used by the United States over imports of tires in September 2009), the vast majority of the increase in TTB product coverage came through antidumping (*black dashed* line).

Figure 3b further decomposes the black and grey lines of Figure 3a – i.e., the stock and flow series based on all TTBs – into whether the policy-imposing economy was a developed or developing G20 member. The result shows that the main *source* of the overall increase in the stock of product coverage during the

2008–09 crisis was new TTBs imposed by *developing* economies, which combined to have 40 per cent more products subject to a TTB in 2009 (2.55 per cent of their imported HS-06 products) than before the crisis in 2007 (1.71 per cent of their imported HS-06 products). On the other hand, developed economies combined to have only 5 per cent more products subject to a TTB in 2009 (1.71 per cent of their imported HS-06 products) than before the crisis in 2007 (1.63 per cent of their imported HS-06 products).

The second important point coming out of Figure 3b is that it is difficult to rule out visually that the relative changes in the data between 2007 and 2009 are not simply part of a longer-term trend in TTB use and thus are *unrelated* to the crisis. Put differently, it will be difficult to conclude that the 40 per cent increase in developing economy product coverage subject to TTBs was *caused by* the crisis. Because of the precrisis upward trend for developing economy users, the 40 per cent increase may have taken place even under more 'normal' macroeconomic conditions had the 2008–09 crisis not occurred.

I address this question more closely in Table 3. In addition to summarising Figure 3, Table 3 also provides a breakdown, by policy-imposing G20 economy, of the percentage change in the stock of product coverage of TTBs between 2007 and 2009 using both the counts [column (1)] and values [column (4)] methods. The economies are ordered in the table by which had the largest percentage change in TTB product coverage between 2007 and 2009 using the *count* method. Three major emerging economies – India, Indonesia and Argentina – lead the list with the largest increases in the stocks of products covered by TTBs during this period, again reflecting the information presented in Figure 2.

The main piece of new data presented in Table 3 are economy-by-economy *forecasts* of the 2009 level of TTB coverage based on predictions from the historical data. Motivated by Figure 3b, the thought experiment is simply to regress the 1997–2007 import share data on a linear time trend, use the estimated coefficient from the regression to *predict* the (out of sample) import share for 2009 and then to compare the prediction for 2009 with the realised data for 2009. I report in column (3) the prediction that uses the *count* measure, and I report in column (6) the prediction that uses the *value* measure.

Table 3 comparison of column (2) with (3) and column (5) with (6) makes it difficult to conclude that the change in product coverage taking place between 2007 and 2009 is a substantial deviation from historical trends. First note that in columns (2) and (5), I make bold all realisations of the 2009 import share data that were *larger than* the 2009 predicted import share stemming from the simple linear regression model. According to the *count* measure, 10 economies (five developing and five developed) had a larger share of 2009 imports become subject to TTBs than was predicted from the models. Only four economies (China, South Africa, Mexico and South Korea) had less product coverage by 2009 than was predicted. On the other hand, using the *value* measure and comparing column (5)

CHAD P. BOWN

TABLE 3
The Crisis: Predicted vs. Realised G20 Economies' Stocks of Imposed Temporary
Trade Barriers in 2009

G20 Economy Imposer (Ranked by Column 1)	Per cent Change in 2009 Import Share Relative to Precrisis 2007 Level, by Count (1)	2009 Import Share, by Count (2)	Predicted 2009 Import Share, by Count (3)	Per cent Change in 2009 Import Share Relative to Precrisis 2007 Level, by Value (4)	2009 Import Share, by Value (5)	Predicted 2009 Import Share, by Value (6)
Total	25.42	**2.15**	1.88	–	–	–
Developing economy total	39.75	**2.55**	2.14	–	–	–
India	69.69	**6.09**	4.28	39.14	**2.94**	2.62
Indonesia	67.25	**0.49**	0.26	108.69	**0.68**	0.29
Argentina	48.01	**2.81**	2.12	18.66	2.01	2.36
Turkey	34.39	**5.31**	4.36	−9.25	3.05	3.35
Brazil	20.03	**1.53**	1.27	−13.57	1.73	2.49
China	−10.03	0.87	1.65	−28.75	1.71	3.91
South Africa	−18.54	0.76	1.00	−60.57	0.25	0.51
Mexico	−287.94	1.09	18.98	−31.81	0.68	0.76
High-income economy total	4.90	**1.71**	1.60	–	–	–
Japan	40.68	**0.06**	0.02	0.44	**1.06**	0.79
Australia	39.64	**0.60**	0.33	69.17	**0.40**	0.12
Canada	15.68	**1.27**	1.19	21.04	**0.64**	0.59
United States	10.17	**4.72**	4.63	0.11	**2.33**	1.80
European Union	−4.98	**2.50**	2.37	−58.04	1.59	2.66
South Korea	−36.39	0.86	0.92	−14.33	0.39	0.45

Notes:
(i) Column (2) is computed using Appendix equation (A1) and column (5) uses equation (A2).
(ii) Predictions for 2009 in columns (3) and (6) are generated from the coefficients resulting from a regression of 1997–2007 annual import share measures that use the 'count' and 'value' approaches, respectively, on a linear time trend. Bold denotes all realisations of the 2009 import share data that were larger than the 2009 predicted import share stemming from the simple linear regression model.

Source: Compiled by the author from the Temporary Trade Barriers Database (Bown, 2010a), imports data from *Comtrade*. Column (2) is computed using equation (A1) and column (5) uses equation (A2). Predictions for 2009 in columns (3) and (6) are generated from the coefficients resulting from a regression of 1997–2007 annual import share measures that use the 'count' and 'value' approaches, respectively, on a linear time trend.

with (6) gives different results; only six economies (two developing and four developed) had a higher-thanpredicted share of imports become subject to TTBs by 2009. While these economies (India, Indonesia, Australia, Canada, US, Japan) did experience increases in the share of imported products subject to TTBs during the economic crisis [see column (4)], the simple linear time trend model predicted this. Therefore, it is only the small *difference* between the realised 2009 data and the 2009 forecast that is the unpredicted piece of new import protection that one could associate with being related to the crisis. According to column (6), Argentina actually experienced a smaller increase in imports covered by TTBs in 2009 than the time trend model predicts– i.e., not controlling for any of the sizable macroeconomic changes during the recession which would make conditions even more likely for an increase in TTBs. Turkey's *value* measure fell slightly (−9.25 per cent) in 2009 compared to 2007 according to column (4), despite the model predicting a slight increase from the 2007 realised value.[19]

Thus, while there was an increase in import protection during the crisis – at least as measured by the stock of imported products subject to TTBs in 2009 being higher than in 2007 – my interpretation of the preliminary evidence is that it is difficult to support a claim that the increase was *caused by* the crisis, given underlying, precrisis trends already apparent in the data.

4. EXPORTERS AND FOREIGN USE OF ANTIDUMPING

In this section, I switch focus to the *incidence* of TTB policies, and I ultimately take the perspective of the exporters directly and negatively impacted by imposed TTBs. Furthermore, in this section, I restrict my attention to the antidumping policy instrument.

I structure this section in two parts.[20] In the first subsection, I examine the use of antidumping from the perspective of each G20 policy-imposing economy to identify trends and potential heterogeneity in the application of the policy across different categories of foreign export targets. In the second subsection, I re-orient the analysis to the perspective of the exporters themselves. This allows me to examine the frequency with which their exported products are targeted by foreign use of antidumping over time.

a. Foreign Targets and Developed Versus Developing Economy Users of Antidumping

Figure 4 presents cumulative annual G20 stocks of 'count' of the *combination* of HS-06 products and foreign trading partners affected by imposed antidumping

---

[19] The substantial difference between the realised import shares for Turkey in 2009 based on the count versus value measures merits an explanation. While Turkey increased (on net) the number of HS-06 products subject to TTBs in 2009 relative to 2007, the particular HS-06 products for which Turkey removed TTBs during this period were such a large share of imports that the value measure declined slightly. The products were associated with Turkey's removal of antidumping barriers on sizable imports of steel billets from Russia, Ukraine and Moldova that had been in effect since 1995.
[20] In this section of the paper, and for reasons described above (see again Figure 2a), Mexico is the only major G20 user of such policies not included in the construction of data behind Figures 4–7 and Table 5.

FIGURE 4

Exporters Affected by G20 Use of Antidumping

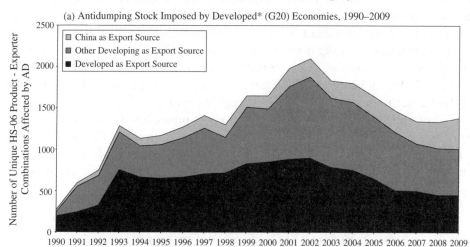

(a) Antidumping Stock Imposed by Developed* (G20) Economies, 1990–2009

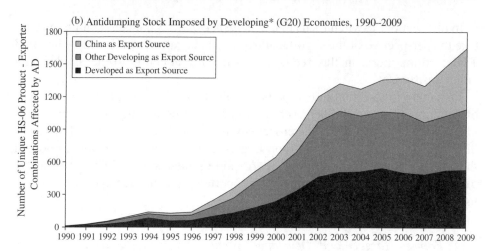

(b) Antidumping Stock Imposed by Developing* (G20) Economies, 1990–2009

Notes:

*The policies are separately aggregated over six developed G20 economy users (Australia, Canada, European Union, Japan, South Korea and United States) and seven developing G20 economy users (Argentina, Brazil, China, India, Indonesia, South Africa and Turkey). Mexico is the only major G20 user of such policies not included for reasons described in the text (see again Figure 2).

Source: Calculated using a modified version of Appendix equation (A1), in which I focus only on the numerator (dropping the denominator), using data in the Temporary Trade Barriers Database (Bown, 2010a). The figures illustrate the annual count of importing country-product-exporting country target combinations affected by the imposition of antidumping.

barriers over time.[21] Here, the figure splits the analysis into two groups of policy-imposing economies – Figure 4a is the developed economy members of the G20, and Figure 4b is the developing economy members. Each panel's stock of product-trading partner combinations subject to antidumping is subsequently decomposed into three categories of exporting economy targets: China, other developing economies (non-China), and developed economies.

The cumulative stock of product-trading partner combinations subject to antidumping (illustrated in Figure 4) tracks the time trends of Figure 3b (which includes TTB-affected products, but did not count affected trading partners) quite closely. Developed economy users of antidumping have seen their cumulative stock affected by antidumping fall over time, and the level by 2009 is well below the within-period peak of the previous 15 years, which took place around 2002–03.[22] On the other hand, as of 2009, the developing economy users of antidumping are still adding to their stocks of product-trading partner combinations subject to antidumping.

Consider next the decomposition of which trading partners are affected by each policy-imposing group's use of antidumping. For the developed economy stock of imports that remains affected by antidumping, over time, the incidence has increasingly shifted away from developed economy exporters and towards China and other developing economy exporters. Specifically compare 1997 with 2009. In 1997, 50 per cent of the developed economy stock of AD was imposed against other developed economies, 11 per cent was imposed against China, and 39 per cent was imposed against other (non-China) developing economies. By 2009, developed economies imposed only 33 per cent of the stock of AD against each other (developed economies); by contrast, developed economies imposed 27 per cent against China and 41 per cent against other (non-China) developing

---

[21] Construction of Figure 4 uses a modified version of Appendix equation (A1). Instead of examining counts of HS-06 products normalised by the set of the economy's total imported HS-06 products, I construct the measure by using counts of *combinations* of HS-06 products and foreign trading partners. Furthermore, I report the measure as a simple count and not as a share of (say) the economy's entire set of HS-06 imported product and foreign trading partner combinations. Specifically, whereas one HS-06 product would be counted once in equation (A1) regardless of how many trading partners were simultaneously subject to an antidumping barrier over that product, this measure adjusts for the number of trading partners subject to the barrier. For example, the AD on one HS-06 product imposed on three trading partners would receive an entry of three in the count measure used in Figure 4.

[22] As I hint at elsewhere in the paper, this is a combination of two factors. First, there are fewer HS-06 products covered by the stock of imposed AD in 2009 than in earlier years. Second, the newest imposed AD on any given HS-06 product is more likely to be imposed on one foreign export source (e.g. China) than in the past, and especially with respect to the products being removed from the previous year's stock after Sunset Reviews. Antidumping imposed over a 6-digit HS product in the 1990s or early 2000s (and thus the products for which AD is being removed in the mid-to-late 2000s) was more likely to have been imposed against *multiple* foreign sources. Bown (2010c) documents how the rate at which a single country (e.g. China) is named in AD cases has risen over time.

economies. Table 4 summarises the implications of Figure 4, and it also presents this same data decomposition for each of the G20 policy-imposing economies individually.

For the developing economies, the changing pattern to the exporter incidence of antidumping is even stronger. By 2009, not only are developing economies still adding to their stocks of product-trading partner combinations targeted by anti-dumping, but also the incidence of this antidumping is increasingly concentrated on *other* developing economies' exports. Overall, 61 per cent of antidumping use by developing economies targeted other developing economies by 2002, and this grew to 68 per cent by 2009. There is also a trend within developing economies to increasingly focus their use of antidumping to specifically address imports from China: 34 per cent of their antidumping use by 2009 was against China, and this is notably higher than both *developed* economy use against China by 2009 (27 per cent) and what *developing* economy use against China was by 2002 (19 per cent). Table 4 also illustrates the substantial heterogeneity in the exporter incidence across the policy-imposing economies. In 2009, Turkey, Brazil and India each targeted China with 40 per cent or more of the stock of product – trading partner combinations that were affected by antidumping. The two notable exceptions to the trend in the increased concentration of antidumping targeting imports of China are Mexico (discussed above) and Japan (a relatively small user of the policy overall).

Finally, for all of the attention focused on the United States use of antidumping, it is worth pointing out that China was affected by *only* 21 per cent of the stock of product – trading partner combinations targeted by a US antidumping barrier by 2009. This is the *lowest* share of all of the developed economy G20 members users of antidumping. Nevertheless, this figure for the United States has increased from 8 per cent in 1997 and from only 10 per cent as late as 2002.

b. Antidumping From the Exporter's Perspective

While China and other developing economies are increasingly the target of the antidumping barriers that are in place, how important are such trade barriers from the perspective of their total exports? Given that China and a number of other emerging economies have exports that have expanded considerably under both the intensive margin (increased growth in volumes of existing products) and extensive margin (entry into new product markets), use of antidumping could be but a nui-sance and perhaps a small price they are willing to pay for trading partners' will-ingness to accommodate their overall export expansion.

To begin to address these questions, I re-orient the analysis and consider the perspective of the exporting economies that send their products to these G20 import markets that have been my focus thus far. I structure my empirical analysis around a simple modification of the 'count' method defined explicitly in Appendix

TABLE 4

The Shifting Incidence of G20 Economies' Annual Stock of Imports Subject to Antidumping

G20 Economy Imposer (Ranked by Column 1)	2009			2002			1997		
	Against China (1)	Against Other Developing (2)	Against Developed (3)	Against China (4)	Against Other Developing (5)	Against Developed (6)	Against China (7)	Against Other Developing (8)	Against Developed (9)
Developing economies[a]	34.10	33.62	32.28	19.19	42.28	38.54	24.10	34.54	41.37
Turkey	48.25	33.96	17.79	46.53	27.72	25.74	12.50	43.75	43.75
Brazil	46.08	26.47	27.45	17.50	40.00	42.50	23.81	38.10	38.10
India	39.76	21.88	38.37	16.58	34.18	49.23	25.64	25.64	48.72
South Africa	33.90	45.76	20.34	20.15	42.54	37.31	24.10	15.66	60.24
Argentina	21.93	55.56	22.51	6.83	64.16	29.01	50.00	27.27	22.73
Mexico	20.00	40.00	40.00	94.05	2.47	3.48	90.63	3.71	5.66
Indonesia	18.18	56.06	25.76	19.30	61.40	19.30	22.22	77.78	0.00
China	na	15.91	84.09	0.00	15.22	84.78	na	na	na
High-income economies	26.78	40.86	32.37	10.62	46.71	42.67	10.84	39.24	49.93
Australia	44.19	20.93	34.88	8.33	50.00	41.67	10.00	28.57	61.43
European Union	42.39	42.80	14.81	15.54	57.77	26.69	14.90	72.57	12.53
South Korea	29.33	29.33	41.33	21.74	17.39	60.87	20.00	8.57	71.43
Canada	26.50	44.02	29.49	9.65	51.54	38.81	8.15	17.39	74.46
Japan	25.00	25.00	50.00	na	na	na	100.00	0.00	0.00
United States	20.80	41.59	37.61	9.89	43.27	46.84	8.19	24.73	67.07

Note:
[a] Not including Mexico as a policy-imposing economy, for reasons described in the text (see again Figure 2).

Source: Compiled by the author from the Temporary Trade Barriers Database (Bown, 2010a) and computed using equation (A1).

108   CHAD P. BOWN

equation (A1). Now instead of constructing measures of how antidumping trade barriers affect the share of the stock of an importing economy's total set of imported products, I focus on the share of the exporting economy's stock of exported products sent to the G20 that are subsequently subject to foreign (G20) use of antidumping.

Begin with Figures 5 and 6, which present my first results that focus on the G20 developing economies from their perspectives as *exporters* concerned with the share of their stock of exported products subject to foreign-imposed antidumping barriers. Each panel in the figure provides two series of data derived from a modified version of the count measure. The black solid line starts with the total count of HS-06 exported products sent to the G20 *developing* economies (denominator) and reports the share of those products subject to a G20 developing economy-imposed antidumping barrier that year. The dashed line with circles starts with the total count of HS-06 exported products sent to the G20 *developed* economies (denominator) and reports the share of those products subject to a G20 developed economy-imposed antidumping barrier that year.

To interpret Figures 5 and 6, consider the case of China's exports. Just prior to China's WTO accession in 2000, China's exports faced antidumping at about the same rate, regardless of whether they were intended to developing or developed economy markets. Just under 1 per cent of its exports to developing economies and just under 1 per cent of its exports to developed economies were subject to antidumping barriers imposed by governments in those markets. Since the 2001 WTO accession, an increasing share of China's exported product categories have been targeted by foreign antidumping, though the rate of increase is much higher for its exports sent to developing economies. By 2009, 2.61 per cent of all Chinese HS-06 products exported to other *developing* economies were subject to a foreign antidumping barrier. The share of China's exports to developing economies that became subject to antidumping has nearly *tripled* in the 10 years since 2000. On the other hand, only 1.55 per cent of China's exported products to developed economies were subject to foreign antidumping by 2009.

It is also important to note that the rate at which China is increasingly being targeted with foreign antidumping is taking place despite China's continued export growth during this period, including its expansion into new markets. These are factors that would expectedly increase the *level* (number of instances) in which China is targeted with AD and is a measure that I report below in Table 5. China has not only seen an increase in the level of instances hit with foreign antidumping, but it has also seen a rapid increase in the *share* of its overall exported product count that is being affected over time.

Turning away from China, Figure 5 also illustrates substantial heterogeneity across the developing economy exporters as to how frequently each is targeted with foreign antidumping over time. For some G20 countries like Argentina, Brazil, Mexico, Russia and Turkey, both the share of exports to developed

FIGURE 5
Developing (G20) Economy Exports and Foreign Antidumping, 1990–2009

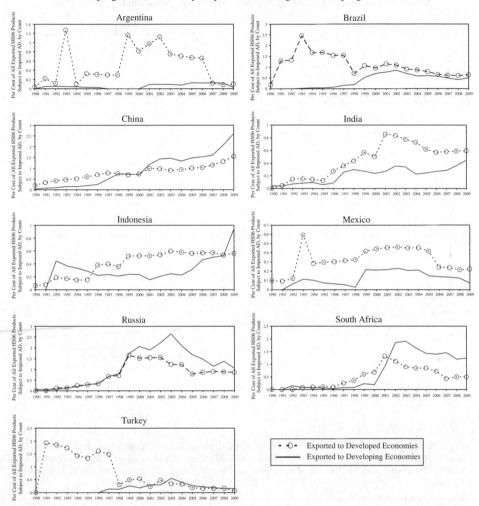

Notes:
The figures illustrate the number of importing country-product combinations affected because of the use of antidumping aggregated over the following G20 economies: seven developing (Argentina, Brazil, China, India, Indonesia, South Africa and Turkey) and six developed (Australia, Canada, the European Union, Japan, South Korea and the United States). Mexico is the only major G20 user of such policies not included in construction of the data for the figures, for reasons explained in the text (see also Figure 2).

Source: Calculated using a modified version of Appendix equation (A1) with data in the Temporary Trade Barriers Database (Bown, 2010a).

FIGURE 6
Developing (non-G20) Economy Exports and Foreign Antidumping, 1990–2009

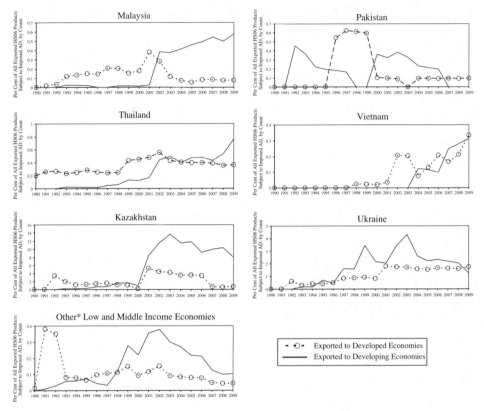

Note:
Other includes Albania, Algeria, Armenia, Azerbaijan, Bangladesh, Belarus, Bosnia and Herzegovina, Chile, Colombia, Cote d'Ivoire, Costa Rica, Cuba, Dominican Republic, Ecuador, Egypt, Georgia, Iran, Kyrgyz Republic, Macedonia, Malawi, Moldova, Nepal, Nigeria, Paraguay, Peru, Philippines, Sri Lanka, Uruguay and Venezuela.
Source: See source notes to Figure 5.

economies targeted by foreign antidumping as well as the overall incidence (the averages of the two series on each panel) have *fallen* dramatically. For other G20 economies like India, Indonesia and South Africa, there have been more recent *increases* to the share of overall exports that are being targeted by foreign anti-dumping. For these economies, most of this is driven by the antidumping imposed by other developing economy members of the G20. This is further evidence of the concern that antidumping is increasingly a 'South–South' phenomenon, and that developing economies face an increasing concern that TTB use erodes poten-tial benefits through applied tariff cuts, binding of those tariffs and nondiscrimina-tory, most-favoured-nation (MFN) treatment embodied in the WTO.

TABLE 5
Exporters' Products Subject to Stock of G20*-Imposed Antidumping Barriers, 2009

Exporting Economy (Ranked by Column 1)	Count of HS-06 Product – G20 Import Market Combinations Subject to AD (1)	Share of all Exported Products to Developing Economies, by Count (2)	Per cent Change in (2) Relative to Precrisis 2007 Level (3)	Share of All Exported Products to Developed Economies, by Count (4)	Per cent Change in (4) Relative to Precrisis 2007 Level (5)
Developing economy exporters					
China	911	2.61	48.34	1.55	30.04
India	150	0.45	46.05	0.60	2.43
Thailand	137	0.76	56.91	0.36	−6.45
Indonesia	129	0.95	63.81	0.56	−2.04
Ukraine	107	1.25	−56.73	1.74	7.53
Brazil	107	0.51	3.14	0.65	4.41
Russia	97	1.05	−9.06	0.86	−5.63
South Africa	91	1.24	−15.77	0.50	15.03
Malaysia	68	0.58	6.13	0.08	−8.81
Vietnam	48	0.31	23.00	0.33	69.31
Kazakhstan	38	7.94	−22.14	0.66	−3.13
Mexico	31	0.07	−64.79	0.22	−6.24
Turkey	17	0.16	−16.39	0.07	−82.08
Argentina	6	0.03	−158.99	0.10	−18.57
Pakistan	5	0.00	0.00	0.09	−0.22
Other developing	59	0.10	−18.51	0.04	−6.87
High-income economy exporters					
South Korea	247	1.07	21.60	0.57	−7.26
European Union	222	0.43	−1.31	0.59	4.55
Taiwan, China	201	0.72	11.33	0.54	2.60
Japan	139	0.29	3.61	0.52	−9.51
United States	91	0.28	20.68	0.12	−33.39
Other high income	85	0.09	2.93	0.04	−23.60

Note:
(i) HS = harmonised system.
(ii) The table documents the number of importing country-product combinations affected because of the use of antidumping aggregated over the following G20 economies: seven developing (Argentina, Brazil, China, India, Indonesia, South Africa and Turkey) and six developed (Australia, Canada, the European Union, Japan, South Korea and the United States). Mexico is the only major G20 user of such policies not included in the computation of the data used to construct the table, for reasons described in the text (see again Figure 2).

Source: Calculated using a modified version of Appendix equation (A1) from data in the Temporary Trade Barriers Database (Bown, 2010a).

Figure 6 provides the same information for other developing economy exporters which are (or have been) considerable targets of G20 antidumping, but which themselves are not members of the G20. Economies like Malaysia, Thailand and Vietnam have seen considerable increases to the share of their exported products, especially to other developing economies, affected by antidumping. Economies

FIGURE 7
Developed Economy Exports and Foreign Antidumping, 1990–2009

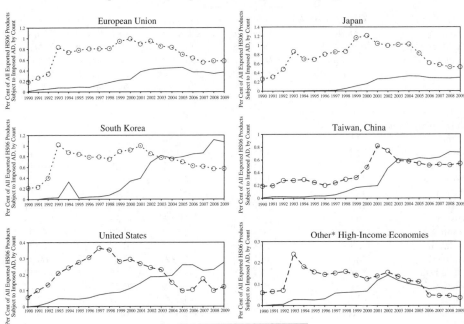

Note:
*Other includes Australia, Canada, Croatia, Hong Kong SAR, China; Israel, Kuwait, Macau SAR, China, Norway, Oman, Qatar, Saudi Arabia, Singapore, Trinidad and Tobago and United Arab Emirates.

Source: See source notes to Figure 5.

like Kazakhstan and Ukraine are notable because there are years in which sizable shares of their exported products to developing economies are targeted by antidumping, heights reached more than 4 per cent for Ukraine and nearly 14 per cent for Kazakhstan. This is partially driven by the fact that these economies export few HS-06 products overall to other developing economies.

Figure 7 presents the same basic information contained in Figures 5 and 6 but from the perspective of the higher-income economies, a number of which were the major targets of antidumping in the 1980s and 1990s. Overall, each of these exporting economies has seen a reduced share of its exports to other *developed* economies being targeted by foreign antidumping. For the antidumping barriers that remain on high-income economy exports, they increasingly stem from the policies imposed by developing economies. Nevertheless, even for the major developed economy exporters, the share of their exports to developing countries that is targeted by foreign antidumping is much smaller than what confronts China, for example, as well as some other developing economy exporters.

Table 5 summarises and expands upon the results of Figures 5–7. First, note that the ordering of the exporting economies is by the count of product-trading partner combinations in which their exports were subject to a foreign antidumping barrier in 2009.[23] As already indicated, China's exports are first on the list, with nearly four times as many product-foreign market combinations being subject to antidumping in 2009 as the next most targeted group of economies (South Korea; EU; Taiwan, China). Two other features of the data that also separate China from these high-income economy exporters are that the *share* of China's exports to developing (column 2) *and* developed (column 4) economies that is being targeted is much higher, and China faces a higher rate of growth at which the targeting of its exports has been increasing over time. While Figures 5–7 illustrate this over a longer time horizon, columns (3) and (5) report the growth (between 2007 and 2009) of the share of the exporting economy's exported products that are targeted by foreign antidumping, as imposed by developing and developed trading partners separately. For China, the share of exported products to developing countries subject to antidumping grew by 48 per cent between 2007 and 2009, and the share of exported products to developed countries subject to antidumping grew by 30 per cent.

Column (3) reveals that developing economy exporters such as India, Thailand, Indonesia and Vietnam share another common tie with China – i.e., substantial growth in the share of their stock of exported products to *developing* economy trading partners becoming subject to TTBs during the crisis. China's increased coverage of 48 per cent between 2007 and 2009 was surpassed by the increases facing Thailand (57 per cent) and Indonesia (64 per cent) and followed by India (46 per cent) and Vietnam (23 per cent). South Korea (22 per cent) and the United States (21 per cent) also saw substantial increases in the share of their exported products to developing economies become subject to foreign antidumping during the crisis, though, in the case of the United States, it started from a much lower baseline share of affected exports in 2007 relative to most of these other economies.

5. COUNTERVAILING DUTIES AND SUBSIDIES BEFORE AND AFTER THE CRISIS

The rules governing the use of CVDs allow the imposition of new trade barriers to offset the allocation of foreign government subsidies to firms that export products that subsequently injure import-competing industries in another market. Like

---

[23] Again to be clear, this is the stock of products subject to antidumping barriers in effect in 2009 and *not* only the barriers that were newly imposed in 2009.

the antidumping law, economists have questioned the implementation of CVD provisions into trade agreements like the WTO, as well as trade agreement rules limiting the national imposition of subsidies more broadly (Bagwell and Staiger, 2006; Ruta et al., 2009). Regardless of whether use of or rules governing CVDs are economically sensible, understanding the extent of CVD use is economically important.

Furthermore, a number of recent political-economic events coincided to increase the likelihood that CVD use is on an upward trend. First, the 2007 US reversal of its mid-1980s *Georgetown Steel* decision has resulted in a policy shift so that the United States now accepts domestic petitions to apply CVDs against imports from China. After more than 20 years of refusing to consider imposition of CVDs against imports from nonmarket economies, the change resulted in the United States applying duties on Chinese imports after 17 separate investigations between 2007 and 2009. Second, a number of other WTO member economies have also either recently implemented new CVD legislation thus expanding their TTB policy arsenal (India, China, Turkey), or they have joined the United States and also started to use CVDs against China after having previously declined to do so (Australia, Canada, European Union). Third, given that many economies are now willing to consider CVD use against China, the long-standing concern with the value of China's currency and that it can act as an implicit export subsidy may also fuel increased CVD use.[24] Fourth, when access to the China-specific transitional safeguard and China's nonmarket economy status under antidumping expires after 2013–14, countries will have less discretion with respect to how they use *other* TTB policies against China's exports which may push policymakers to use alternative TTB instruments like CVDs. Fifth, the 2008–09 crisis resulted in a number of WTO members bailing out sizable domestic industries; the Global Trade Alert (Evenett, 2009) documents dozens of such subsidies since November 2008. The Global Trade Alert lacks comparable data on bailouts and subsidy packages from *before* the crisis to assess whether the identification of 2008–09 subsidies is any more or less than previous use. Nevertheless, based on anecdotal evidence of the CVD response after earlier financial crises (e.g. multiple economies imposing CVDs on sizable imports of Korean semiconductors after the Korean bailout of Hynix during the Asian crisis), there may be cause to expect more CVD use after the 2008–09 crisis.[25]

Figure 8a, b illustrate the use of CVDs over 1990–2009 by the United States and all other G20 policy-imposing economies, respectively. The figures adopt the

---

[24] Staiger and Sykes (2010) provide a notable critique of the hypothesised link between China's exchange rate undervaluation and export subsidisation, and whether any such link could be addressed through CVDs.

[25] Indeed, China's first CVD case was against the United States over Grain-Oriented Electrical Steel (GOES), and it alleges injurious subsidies in 'Buy America' provisions associated with the 2009 US stimulus package.

FIGURE 8
G20 Use of Countervailing Duties (CVD) (with and without AD), 1990–2009

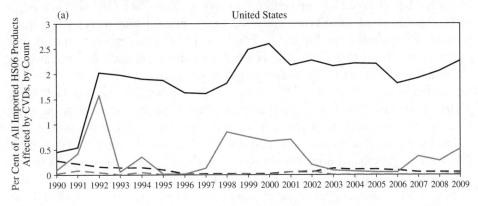

(a)   United States

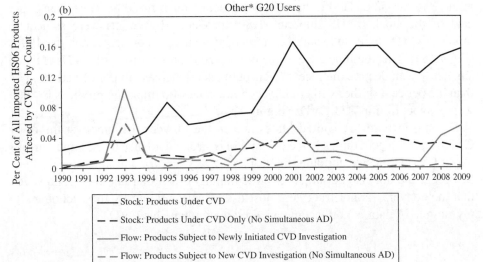

(b)   Other* G20 Users

——— Stock: Products Under CVD

— — Stock: Products Under CVD Only (No Simultaneous AD)

——— Flow: Products Subject to Newly Initiated CVD Investigation

— — Flow: Products Subject to New CVD Investigation (No Simultaneous AD)

Notes:
*The data are aggregated over the following 10 other G20 economies: Argentina, Australia, Brazil, Canada, China, the European Union, India, Japan, Mexico and Turkey. The only major G20 user of CVDs not included in the figure is South Africa, for data availability reasons.

Source: Calculated using a modified version of equation (A1) from data in the Temporary Trade Barriers Database (Bown, 2010a). *The data are aggregated over the following 10 other G20 economies: Argentina, Australia, Brazil, Canada, China, the European Union, India, Japan, Mexico and Turkey. The only major G20 user of CVDs not included in the figure is South Africa, for data availability reasons.

'count' measure of the share of imported products subject to the TTB (in this case the CVD) over time. However, I define the data series of interest differently from the earlier figures, based on my observation of how CVDs are being used in practice. In a number of economies, policymakers use CVDs *simultaneously* with antidumping. For example, the government initiates a simultaneous investigation under both its AD and CVD law of firms from the same foreign country over imports of the same HS-06 product, responding to a domestic industry's allegation that it has been injured by dumped imports that also received GATT/WTO-illegal foreign government subsidies. Figure 8a, b each present four pieces of information. In each panel of the figure, the *black solid* line represents the annual stock of products subject to a CVD. The *black dashed* line represents the annual stock of products subject to a CVD that are *not* also subject to a simultaneous antidumping action – i.e., where the CVD policy is not 'redundant' (in producttrading partner coverage, though not necessarily in terms of the size of the duty imposed, an issue I do not address here). Similarly, the *grey solid* and *grey dashed* lines reflect the annual *flow* of products subject to all CVD investigations and only those CVD investigations without simultaneous antidumping, respectively. There are two main sets of implications to draw from Figure 8.

First, CVDs have a larger scope of import product coverage in the United States relative to the other G20 policy-imposing economies. In 2009, more than 2 per cent of the stock of US imported HS06 products (by count) were subject to imposed CVDs, and this share has remained relatively constant since the 1990s (Figure 8a). The combined use of the other G20 economy users of CVDs is much smaller – even despite the recent (well-publicised) increase in policy activity, less than 0.2 per cent of these other G20 economies' HS-06 imported products in 2009 were subject to imposed CVDs (Figure 8b).[26]

Second, in both the United States and in the broader use amongst the other CVD-imposing economies in the G20, there is strong evidence of the simultaneous use of CVD alongside antidumping. It is relatively rare for a product to be subject to a CVD and not also be subject to antidumping. It is important to note, however, that the converse is not true; i.e., most use of antidumping by the economies in my sample of data is not accompanied by a simultaneous CVD.

6. CONCLUSIONS AND NEW DIRECTIONS FOR RESEARCH

This paper examines the evolving, cross-country use of temporary trade barriers (TTBs) – antidumping, safeguard and countervailing duty policies – during 1990–2009. I construct new measures of annual, product-level stocks and flows of these

---

[26] Furthermore, the United States has been and remains the dominant user of CVDs. While not shown in the figure, I can also confirm that the United States was responsible for roughly 50 per cent of the stock of entire HS-06 products that the G20 imported that were subject to CVDs during this period. The other G20 economies combined to contribute the other 50 per cent. The other G20 users of CVD (shown in the lower panel of Figure 8) are Argentina, Australia, Brazil, Canada, China, EU, India, Japan, Mexico and Turkey. According to the WTO, South Africa also has some use of CVDs, but I am unable to identify the HS-06 product codes associated with its use because of lack of publically available information.

TTBs with newly available data drawn from the World Bank's *Temporary Trade Barriers Database*.

I benchmark trends in historical use and establish a number of facts regarding use of the TTB policies to measure any changes in import protection taking place during the global economic crisis of 2008–09. I find that the 2008–09 economic shock mostly accentuates patterns already visible in the precrisis data. While the major G20 users of such policies combined to increase the stock of product lines subject to TTBs by 25 per cent during the crisis, most of this is the result of developing economies that combined to increase their stock of product coverage by 40 per cent. Perhaps surprisingly, high-income economies increased their stock of products affected by TTBs by only 5 per cent during the crisis.

Furthermore, these changes during the global economic crisis are consistent with precrisis trends in the data on TTB use. Developing countries have been increasing their use of TTBs prior to the crisis at such a rate that it is difficult to claim empirically that the 2008–09 crisis *caused* developing economies to increase their stock of TTBs above what the simple time trend would predict even in the absence of a major global recession. On the other hand, the United States and EU have reduced the stock of imported products they subject to TTBs by up to 50 per cent over the last 15 years, which is consistent with the crisis data, indicating a muted response to political calls for new TTBs.

Also significant are the trends in the data from the perspective of the exporting economies. By 2009, China had roughly four times as many products subject to foreign-imposed TTBs as the second most targeted economies. Furthermore, the share of China's exports to other *developing* economies is subject to much more foreign-imposed TTBs than its share of exports to developed economies, and it is also growing at a faster rate. My evidence confirms that this particular feature is not unique to China but is shared by a number of other major developing economy exporters, thus deepening the concern that such discriminatory trade barriers are increasingly a 'South–South' phenomenon.

Finally, I conclude by commenting on how the lack of a substantial increase in new import protection resulting from the 2008–09 crisis beyond that predicted from precrisis data raises important questions for research. If the world trading system does ultimately escape the 2008–09 crisis relatively unscathed with respect to new and extraordinary protectionist initiatives, an open and fundamentally important question is, why?

These facts on TTB use and nonuse during the 2008–09 crisis suggest many potential contributing causes that should form the basis for future research. One is that the WTO architecture was well constructed to handle the crisis; perhaps a system that permits TTB use allowed domestic political pressure for new trade barriers to escape via a 'safety valve'. These relatively small (in product coverage terms) though nontrivial increases in import protection may have prevented emergence of greater market-closing forces. On the other hand, the lack of a major protectionist response may be unrelated to WTO rules; it could be a result of the political economy of trade policy changing in a way that actually makes the WTO redundant (Blanchard, 2010). With the proliferation of foreign direct investment and global supply chains, perhaps the traditional model of import-competing industries lobbying for protection is less important. Firms are not only import-competing, but they also rely on imports for components; they export, and thus they are substantially more exposed and invested in keeping markets open. Further still, perhaps preferential trade agreements (PTAs) dampened the incentive to impose new trade barriers. Policymakers may have known that with PTAs, the most accessible forms of new import protection might not even benefit domestic industries, but instead favour PTA partners through trade diversion. Finally, perhaps developed economies with resources to implement fiscal stimulus and industry bailouts used alternative (and arguably more efficient than trade policy) subsidy policies to address the political pressure that, in earlier eras, may have resulted in new trade barriers.

Finally, notwithstanding the insights generated by the crisis, the data on hetero-geneity in TTB use across countries and over time combined with the current trading system of low average applied tariffs reveal the need for more research. What are the implications for the theory of trade agreements (Bagwell and Staiger, 2002) and the design of liberal trade 'exceptions' embodied in their rules? Furthermore, the data reveal exporter incidence of the imposed TTBs to be exten-sive *discriminatory* treatment, especially in the form of 'South–South' protection, and this raises a number of questions for the world trading system and the role of MFN treatment in particular (Ludema and Mayda, 2009). Perhaps at the forefront is the question of whether the resulting patterns of discriminatory protection embodied in TTBs enhance or reduce existing differences in tariff treatment that were caused by previously negotiated preferential trade agreements (Limão, 2006; Estevadeordal et al., 2008). Furthermore, there is also the causal question of whether the changing economic incentives induced by preferential trade agree-ments themselves change the scope of how TTBs are applied.

APPENDIX A: METHODOLOGY

My first methodological approach takes an importing economy's set of HS-06 products as the unit of observation and builds from Bown and Tovar (2011, Figure 1). More formally, let k be the policy-imposing (importing) economy and let $m_{i,t}^k \in \{0,1\}$ be an indicator for whether the economy had nonzero imports of product i in year t. The HS-06 product i is in the economy's time-varying set of HS-06 products with nonzero imports, defined as I_t^k. Next, let $b_{i,t}^k \in \{0,1\}$ be an indicator for whether the importing economy k 'applies' a TTB on imports of product i in year t. Thus, I define my first 'count' measure of the share of annual stock of economy k imported products subject to a TTB as

$$\frac{\sum_{I_t^k} b_{i,t}^k m_{i,t}^k}{\sum_{I_t^k} m_{i,t}^k}. \tag{A1}$$

I rely on a variety of definitions for the TTB indicator $b_{i,t}^k$. I may define it as an indicator of the initiation of a TTB *investigation* of product i in year t; alternatively, I may define $b_{i,t}^k$ as the actual application of a barrier (e.g. import duty, quantitative restriction, price undertaking) imposed over product i in year t. Note that when referring to applied barriers, I take the year of imposition as the first year that the barrier was imposed, even if it was only a preliminary barrier and even if that preliminary barrier was subsequently removed after completion of the full investigation. The application of even preliminary barriers can affect trade both directly (raising costs to exporters) and indirectly (increasing uncertainty about future policy).

My second approach refines equation (A1) by replacing the binary indicator variable for imports, $m_{i,t}^k$ with product-level, value of import data and thus *trade-weighting* the $b_{i,t}^k$ indicator by the HS-06 product-level value of imports, $v_{i,j,t}^k$. While I build from equation (A1), I adapt the approach in two ways.

First, I can now redefine my product-specific, time-varying TTB indicator to now be at the *bilateral* level: let $b_{i,j,t}^k \in \{0,1\}$ be an indicator for whether a TTB applies to the economy k imports of product i from exporter j in year t. This modification allows me to address the possibility of heterogeneity across foreign sources in terms of which trading partners are negatively affected by the TTB and which are not.

The second adaptation requires a slightly more detailed explanation. To ultimately create coverage ratios that are comparable within a country *over time*, I must make an assumption on the counterfactual level of economy k imports in t (as well as $t + 1$, etc.) from a supplier j whose exports had been subject to a TTB imposed in an earlier year (e.g. $t - 1$, $t - 2$, etc.) and thus which did not grow at a 'normal' rate in later years (e.g. t, $t + 1$, etc.). To determine the counterfactual level of imports for such products, I make the simple and conservative assumption that, beginning in year t, yearly imports of TTB-impacted products would have grown *at the same rate* as the economy's non-TTB-impacted products.[27] To make this clear, I decompose the set of economy k imported products I^k into two subsets.

---

[27] There are arguments to suggest such products may grow at a rate different from other products in the economy. For example, these are products that typically had been growing at rates faster than the average rate of import growth, perhaps because of a technological innovation or productivity improvement, and thus one might expect that to have continued. On the other hand, if the imports were growing at faster rates because they were dumped or subsidised (and if the dumping or subsidisation had terminated), one might expect the rate of growth to fall (if the dumping or subsidising stopped), even in the absence of the TTB. While acknowledging the range of theoretical arguments for counterfactual import growth, to construct these measures, I rely on the conservative assumption of TTB-impacted imports growing at the same rate as imports not impacted by TTBs.

Define the first subset as $\hat{I}^k$ and allow it to contain those HS-06 products i subject to a TTB imposed during the sample and for which I need to construct *counter-factual* import values, defined as $\hat{v}^k_{i,j,t}$, for all years that the TTB is in effect. I define the second subset of products as I^{*k} and allow it to contain all (other) imported HS-06 products i which were never subject to an imposed TTB and for which I do *not* need to construct counterfactual import values, and thus for which I can rely on the observable import data $v^k_{i,j,t}$.[28] This modification also addresses the well-known concern that any TTB policy imposed in year t may reduce the (contemporaneous) year t value of imports, and this would underweight the economic importance of the trade barrier in the averaging.

My second measure of the share of annual stock of economy k imported products subject to a TTB in year t, reflecting the three modifications to equation (A1) and thus weighted by the 'value' of imports, is defined as

$$\frac{\sum_{I^k_t} b^k_{i,j,t} \hat{v}^k_{i,j,t}}{\sum_{\hat{I}^k_t} \hat{v}^k_{i,j,t} + \sum_{I^{*k}_t} v^k_{i,j,t}}. \tag{A2}$$

There are at least three other and more subtle transmission mechanisms through which (A1) and (A2) can diverge beyond ways through which I have identified trade-weighting the HS-06 products as leading to differences between the two series. First, defining the series according to the stock of covered HS-06 products prevents the case of a product already subject to a TTB in $t - 1$ from being double counted if a new TTB is imposed over the same product in subsequent years (e.g. in year t). For example, suppose a HS-06 product from a given foreign trading partner became subject to an AD barrier in $t - 1$ and then a CVD in t. Since I am measuring the 'stock' of products affected by TTBs, this would not result in a change to series (A1) or (A2) between $t - 1$ and t. On the other hand, if there is a *new* trading partner being subject to the TTB between $t - 1$ and t, even if the underlying product is unchanged, there can be a change in series (A2). A change in trading partner coverage could occur because either the second partner was targeted under a different underlying TTB policy instrument (e.g. AD vs. CVD) or because of differences in the timing under the same policy instrument (e.g. the first AD imposed over the HS-06 product was imposed against country A in $t - 1$ and not against country B until t). Third, the stock series can also be affected through differential timing in the *removal* of a previously imposed TTB over the same HS-06 product. For example, if the TTB on trading partner A is removed in $t - 1$, but the TTB on trading partner B is not removed until t, this differential timing in the removal will affect series (A2). However, there will be

---

[28] I use the mean annual growth rate of products from the set I^{*k} in t to construct the counterfactual import levels for the products in $\hat{I}^k$ in t, which I denote $\hat{v}^k_{i,j,t}$.

no change in series (A1) until *all* previously imposed TTBs affecting this product are removed.

I conclude this section with a discussion of five remaining caveats to my approach.

First, some economies impose TTBs at a level of product disaggregation (e.g. HS-08, HS-10) that is finer than the HS-06 level that is my focus. Nevertheless, examination at the HS-06 level is desirable for our context, since HS-06 is the finest level of disaggregation that is both comparable across countries and with available import value data during 1990–2009. While the application of measures using HS-06 data will overstate the trade impact (in the level) for any economy that typically does not cover all sub-products within an HS-06 category, because my measures are defined consistently over time and across trading partners, measurement error is much less of a concern for two of our main questions of interest: *intertemporal changes* (i.e. whether the scope of imported products subject to a country's use of TTBs is increasing or decreasing over time) and the *relative exporter incidence* (i.e. whether certain exporters are relatively more or less frequently targeted than others by the stock of imposed TTBs).

Second, my approach concentrates entirely on the potential first-order impact of TTBs on trade. There is a substantial theoretical and empirical literature from case studies that identifies potentially important second-order effects of TTBs (especially antidumping) on trade flows. Some accentuate the potential negative trade effects beyond what I identify here, while others are offsetting and reduce the overall size of the trade effects. Examples of accentuating effects include downstream impacts, tariff-jumping foreign direct investment and retaliation, while examples of offsetting effects include trade diversion. For a recent discussion and a relatively comprehensive list of such effects, see Vandenbussche and Zanardi (2010); for an excellent survey of the antidumping literature, see Blonigen and Prusa (2003).

Third, even trade-weighting the incidence of TTBs does nothing to address heterogeneity in the size of the imposed trade barriers. Bown (2010c), for example, notes substantial heterogeneity in the size of duties imposed across both policy-imposing economies and across targeted exporters by (within) a policy-imposing country, especially with respect to barriers imposed on imports from China.

Fourth, I also do not address potential heterogeneity to the *form* of the applied TTBs. For example, some economies apply antidumping as ad valorem duties, others may be more likely (or against certain trading partners or over certain imported products) to apply it as a specific duty or a 'price undertaking' in which the exporter voluntarily raises its price above some threshold under the threat of an imposed duty. Global safeguards, on the other hand, are frequently applied as quantitative restrictions such as tariff rate quotas.

Fifth, I also do not address the issue of the likely import demand or export supply responses to the imposed TTBs, because I do not control for import demand or export supply elasticities. For an application of the Overall Trade Restrictiveness Index (OTRI) approach to the global economic crisis of 2008–09, see Kee et al. (2010).

APPENDIX B: DATA

Detailed data on antidumping, CVDs, global safeguards and China-specific safeguards are available from the World Bank's *Temporary Trade Barriers Database* (Bown, 2010a). For antidumping and countervailing duty policies, the data in Bown (2010a) are derived from original government source documents. Each government reports tariff-line product codes that are subject to the investigations, the dates and countries from whom imports are being investigated, and the decisions of whether to impose preliminary and final trade barriers, as well as when they are removed. The data on use of global safeguards and China-specific safeguards are derived from both original government source documents and what they report to the WTO's Committee on Safeguards. Bown (2010a) provides a complete discussion of the data sources, as well as the other information contained in the database that is not utilised in the analysis here.

The tariff-line product codes from Bown (2010a) are then matched to bilateral import data at the 6-digit HS product-level taken from Comtrade via WITS. The following countries had missing years of import data at the HS-06 level: Argentina (1990–92), China (1990–91), Japan (2009), South Korea (2009), United States (1990) and South Africa (1990–91). The 'value' share measures derived throughout the paper are based on nonoil import data only.

Because the composition of the European Union changes between 1990 and 2009 and I am especially interested in recent changes to EU policy against non-members, I define the European Union as being made up of the EU-27 member countries throughout the entire sample. Given that definition, I focus on extra-EU imports and I drop all EU trade policy actions against other (even eventual) EU member states during the time period. For example, an EU antidumping case against Romania in 2002 would be dropped from the sample, since Romania eventually became part of the EU27 in 2007.

REFERENCES

Bagwell, K. and R. W. Staiger (2002), *The Economics of the World Trading System* (Cambridge, MA: MIT Press).
Bagwell, K. and R. W. Staiger (2006), 'Will International Rules on Subsidies Disrupt the World Trading System?', *American Economic Review*, **96**, 3, 877–95.
Baldwin, R. E. (ed.) (2009), *The Great Trade Collapse: Causes, Consequences and Prospects*, VoxEU.org E-book, November.
Baldwin, R. E. and S. J. Evenett (eds.) (2009), *The Collapse of Global Trade, Murky Protectionism, and the Crisis: Recommendations for the G20*, VoxEU.org E-book, March.

Blanchard, E. (2010), 'Reevaluating the Role of Trade Agreements: Does Investment Globalization Make the WTO Obsolete?', *Journal of International Economics*, **82**, 1, 63–72.

Blonigen, B. A. and T. J. Prusa (2003), 'Antidumping', in E. K. Choi and J. Harrigan (eds.), *Handbook of International Trade* (Oxford: Blackwell Publishers), 251–84.

Bown, C. P. (2008), 'The WTO and Antidumping in Developing Countries', *Economics and Politics*, **20**, 2, 255–88.

Bown, C. P. (2009), 'The Global Resort to Antidumping, Safeguards, and other Trade Remedies Amidst the Economic Crisis', in S. J. Evenett, B. M. Hoekman and O. Cattaneo (eds.), *Effective Crisis Response and Openness: Implications for the Trading System* (London: CEPR and World Bank), 91–118.

Bown, C. P. (2010a), 'Temporary Trade Barriers Database', The World Bank, Available at: http://econ.worldbank.org/ttbd/ (accessed 30 July 2010).

Bown, C. P. (2010b), 'First Quarter 2010 Protectionism Data: Requests for New Trade Barriers Fall for Second Consecutive Quarter; Newly Imposed Barriers Also Fall', A Monitoring Report to the Temporary Trade Barriers Database, The World Bank, 25 May.

Bown, C. P. (2010c), 'China's WTO Entry: Antidumping, Safeguards, and Dispute Settlement', in R. C. Feenstra and S. Wei (eds.), *China's Growing Role in World Trade* (Chicago, IL: University of Chicago Press for the NBER), 281–337.

Bown, C. P. and M. A. Crowley (2010), 'China's Export Growth and the China Safeguard: Threats to the World Trading System?', *Canadian Journal of Economics*, **43**, 4, 1353–88.

Bown, C. P. and P. Tovar (2011), 'Trade Liberalization, Antidumping and Safeguards: Evidence from India's Tariff Reform', *Journal of Development Economics*, **96**, 1, 115–25.

Cadot, O., J. de Melo and B. Tumurchudur (2007), 'Anti-Dumping Sunset Reviews: The Uneven Reach of WTO Disciplines', CEPR Working Paper No. 6502, September (London: CEPR).

Egger, P. and D. Nelson (forthcoming), 'How Bad is Antidumping?: Evidence from Panel Data', *The Review of Economics and Statistics*.

Estevadeordal, A., C. Freund and E. Ornelas (2008), 'Does Regionalism Affect Trade Liberalization toward Non-Members?', *Quarterly Journal of Economics*, **123**, 4, 1531–75.

Evenett, S. J. (2009), 'Global Trade Alert: Motivation and Launch', *World Trade Review*, **8**, 4, 607–9.

Fischer, R. and T. J. Prusa (2003), 'Contingent Protection as Better Insurance', *Review of International Economics*, **11**, 5, 745–57.

Gallaway, M., B. A. Blonigen and J. Flynn (1999), 'Welfare Cost of the US Antidumping and Countervailing Duty Law', *Journal of International Economics*, **49**, 2, 211–44.

Hoekman, B. M. and M. M. Kostecki (2009), *The Political Economy of the World Trading System*, 3rd edn (Oxford, UK: Oxford University Press).

Irwin, D. A. (2011), *Peddling Protectionism: Smoot-Hawley and the Great Depression* (Princeton, NJ: Princeton University Press).

Kee, H. L., I. C. Neagu and A. Nicita (2010), 'Is Protectionism on the Rise? Assessing National Trade Policies During the Crisis of 2008', World Bank Working Paper No. 5274, April (World Bank).

Knetter, M. M. and T. J. Prusa (2003), 'Macroeconomic Factors and Antidumping Filings: Evidence from Four Countries', *Journal of International Economics*, **61**, 1, 1–17.

Limão, N. (2006), 'Preferential Trade Agreements as Stumbling Blocks for Multilateral Trade Liberalization: Evidence for the US', *American Economic Review*, **96**, 3, 896–914.

Limão, N. and K. Handley (2010), '*Trade and Investment under Policy Uncertainty: Theory and Firm Evidence*', Working Paper, May (College, MD: University of Maryland).

Ludema, R. D. and A. M. Mayda (2009), 'Do Countries Free Ride on MFN?', *Journal of International Economics*, **77**, 2, 137–50.

Messerlin, P. A. (2004), 'China in the World Trade Organization: Antidumping and Safeguards', *World Bank Economic Review*, **18**, 1, 105–30.

Moore, M. O. (2006), 'An Econometric Analysis of US Antidumping Sunset Review Decisions', *Weltwirtschaftliches Archiv*, **142**, 1, 122–50.

Moore, M. O. and M. Zanardi (2009), 'Does Antidumping Use Contribute to Trade Liberalization in Developing Countries?', *Canadian Journal of Economics*, **42**, 2, 469–95.

Niels, G. and J. Francois (2006), 'Business Cycles, the Exchange Rate, and Demand for Antidumping Protection in Mexico', *Review of Development Economics*, **10**, 3, 388–99.

Prusa, T. J. (2001), 'On the Spread and Impact of Antidumping', *Canadian Journal of Economics*, **34**, 3, 591–611.

Reynolds, K. M. (2009), 'From Agreement to Application: An Analysis of Determinations under the WTO Antidumping Agreement', *Review of International Economics*, **17**, 5, 969–85.

Ruta, M., D. Brou and E. Campanella (2009), '*The Value of Domestic Subsidy Rules in Trade Agreements*', WTO Staff Working Paper ERSD-2009-12, November (Geneva: WTO).

Staiger, R. W. and A. O. Sykes (2010), ''Currency Manipulation' and World Trade', *World Trade Review*, **9**, 4, 583–627.

Staiger, R. W. and F. A. Wolak (1994), 'Measuring Industry-Specific Protection: Antidumping in the United States', *Brookings Papers on Economic Activity: Microeconomics*, 51–118.

de la Torre, L. E. R. and J. G. Gonzalez (2005), 'Antidumping and Safeguard Measures in the Political Economy of Liberalization: The Mexican Case', in J. M. Finger and J. J. Nogués (eds.), *Safeguards and Antidumping in Latin American Trade Liberalization: Fighting Fire with Fire* (New York: World Bank and Palgrave), 205–46.

Vandenbussche, H. and M. Zanardi (2010), 'The Chilling Trade Effects of Antidumping Proliferation', *European Economic Review*, **54**, 6, 760–77.

Zanardi, M. (2004), 'Antidumping: What are the Numbers to Discuss at Doha?', *The World Economy*, **27**, 3, 403–33.

6

Special and Differential Treatment of Developing Countries and Export Promotion Policies under the WTO

Jai S. Mah

1. INTRODUCTION

SEVERAL countries recording rapid economic growth rates for the past half century have pursued an outward-oriented economic development strategy. Outward orientation of those countries is regarded as having contributed to rapid economic growth because of, among other reasons, economies of scale arising from expanded sales opportunities and productivity improvement as a result of more competition.[1] Even if those rapidly growing economies commonly pursued outward orientation, they differ significantly in the degree of government intervention, as the issues of outward orientation and the degree of government intervention are separate (Milner 1990: 2). The city states, especially Hong Kong, have followed market-led outward orientation. The experience of the other rapidly growing non-city-state economies such as South Korea and Taiwan shows that their governments tried aggressively to promote exports during the period of rapid economic growth.

In addition to the benefits of outward orientation, we can also expect the rationale for government-led export promotion in the sense of removing any anti-export bias made by import protection and subsidising the infant exporters, as entering

---

[1] Of course, there is also a view that outward orientation has not been so beneficial to development of developing countries. For instance, Singer (1988: 232) expressed the view that the positive effect of outward orientation has become less evident since the mid-1970s even in the newly industrialising countries.

the new export markets is a difficult and costly activity (Meyer, 1984). We can also consider the strategic trade policy argument. According to this, exports subsidised may pre-empt the international market so that the domestic company receives the monopoly profit, as the foreign competitors not subsidised by the government are driven out (Brander and Spencer, 1985). That is, export promotion by the government can be the first-best policy in such a situation, and an appropriate governmental role would be to transfer resources from 'less productive' toward 'more productive' uses (Wade, 2004: xviii).[2]

The northeast Asian developing economies, for instance, were able to pursue active export promotion especially until the 1980s. The measures taken comprised tax incentives (Falvey and Gemmell, 1990), duty drawback (Wade, 1991), export credit/insurance (Mah and Milner, 2005), provision of export processing zones (EPZs) or special economic zones (Warr, 1990; Mah, 2008), devaluation or depreciation of domestic currency and establishment of export promotion organisations providing trade marketing, information and assisting trade fair (Seringhaus and Rosson, 1990). Until the early 1990s, developing countries were relatively free from trade regulations in the global trading system prohibiting the use of export promotion measures. Meanwhile, as of now, there are many restrictions or even strict prohibition on the developing countries' use of export promotion policies under the WTO system. Considering the different levels of economic development between developed and developing countries, one may wonder whether or not the current WTO system, which strictly regulates the use of export promotion policies by developing countries, is 'fair'.

This paper explains the export promotion measures that can be utilised by developing countries under the current WTO system and compares the WTO Members' proposals on modification of export promotion provisions in the Doha Development Agenda (DDA) negotiations. Then, from the viewpoint of 'distributional fairness', it suggests ways of modifying the special and differential treatment (SDT) provisions applied to exports of developing economies in the Agreement on Subsidies and Countervailing Measures, the Subsidies Code hereafter, of the WTO. Despite the importance of export promotion in economic development, there has been little, if any, work focusing on the SDT of developing countries with respect to export promotion policies in the WTO system. This paper is intended to fill that gap.

The structure of this paper is as follows. Section 2 explains the trade regulations governing export promotion policies, especially those relating to developing

---

[2] We can also consider the costs of the export promotion policies, which include giving up allocation of resources to sectors other than exports, the resource allocational inefficiencies because of the difference between the international price and the domestic price in the subsidising country (Barcelo, 1977), forgone tax revenue in case of tax incentives and ill-performing financial sector in case of provision of excessive financial incentives, as seen in the case of the Korean financial crisis (Mah, 2002).

economies. Section 3 describes proposals made by various members during the DDA negotiations. Section 4 provides suggestions for modifying the current WTO regulations in favour of the export promotion of developing economies. Conclusions are provided in Section 5.

2. WTO REGULATIONS ON EXPORT PROMOTION

a. General Agreement on Tariffs and Trade (GATT)

General Agreement on Tariffs and Trade Article XVI made room for controlling subsidy in general and export subsidy in particular. From 1958, GATT Article XVI.4 prohibited the granting of export subsidies other than that provided to primary products. In 1960, the non-exhaustive list of practices deemed to form export subsidies was drafted by a Working Party in the GATT. Six non-tariff barriers (NTBs) Codes were established as a result of the Tokyo Round in 1979. One of those, the Subsidies Code, included an Illustrative List of export subsidies which prohibited export subsidies, which was reintroduced, with only minor modifications, in the Uruguay Round (UR) Subsidies Code later (Collins-Williams and Salembier, 1996; Adamantopoulos and Akritidis, 2008). However, such prohibition of export subsidies did not bind developing countries until the establishment of the WTO, as the contracting parties were allowed to sign the Tokyo Round NTB Codes voluntarily.

Article VI allows the imposition of countervailing duties (CVDs) as a trade remedy to offset the effect of subsidised imports on domestic producers. If there exists subsidised import, material injury to the domestic industry and causation from the former to the latter, then the government of an importing country may impose CVDs to offset the effect of subsidisation.

The contracting parties did not in effect introduce any element of developing country interest into the original framework, because the original GATT was essentially a contract among developed countries (Wolfe, 2004: 586). Developing and developed countries were treated as equals, and the fundamental principle in the initial framework of the GATT was that rights and obligations were to be applied on an equal basis. There was no SDT provision designed for developing economies. Because of the continuing pressure of developing countries, after the 1954–55 GATT Review Session, GATT Article XVIII was modified to focus on government assistance to economic development and only developing countries could derogate from obligations using provisions in it (Pangetsu, 2000: 1286).

Part IV of GATT on Trade and Development was introduced at the end of the Kennedy Round in 1964. While many of the expressions of Part IV suggest just good intentions rather than obligations, the addition was important as it introduced the principle of 'nonreciprocity' for developing countries (GATT Article XXXVI.8). With the inclusion of Part IV of the GATT, developing countries successfully introduced a concept of 'fairness' into the GATT in the sense of recognising the importance of equity of outcomes rather than just legitimacy of process (Narlikar, 2006: 1016–1017). GATT Article XXXVI in Part IV recognises that export earnings of developing countries can play a vital part in their economic development. It also acknowledges the importance of the diversification of export commodities in economic development, stipulating that:

> The rapid expansion of the economies of the less-developed contracting parties will be facilitated by a diversification of the structure of their economies and the avoidance of an excessive dependence on the export of primary products. (Article XXXVI.5)

According to Pangetsu (2000: 1288), Part IV was only a set of guidelines which essentially did not influence the negotiations in favour of developing countries or result in specific actions. Institutionalising the principle of nonreciprocity further, the UNCTAD passed a resolution in favour of an establishment of a system of preferences. The GATT introduced a waiver to the most-favoured nation (MFN) principle, allowing the generalised system of preferences (GSP) for the next 10 years. The GSP was given a legal basis in 1979 as a result of the Tokyo Round, although developed countries were able to withdraw concessions granted under the GSP unilaterally (Narlikar, 2006: 1017).

The Tokyo Round, which ended in 1979, included the Enabling Clause, entitled Differential and More Favourable Treatment, Reciprocity and Fuller Participation of Developing Countries. It included, for the first time, a mention of special treatment for least developed countries, introducing the two-tier concept of developing economies into the global trading system (Pangetsu, 2000: 1288–1289).

b. The Subsidies Code of the WTO[3]

Subsidised exports relating to manufactured goods trade are currently governed by the UR Subsidies Code in the WTO system. Because of the single undertaking in the UR, all members, regardless of their economic development level, were obliged to accept all agreements in the WTO except for the plurilateral agreements. Any kind of subsidy is regarded as one of the following types: prohibited subsidies; actionable subsidies; and non-actionable subsidies.

Subsidy is defined as a financial contribution by a government or any public body and a benefit to be thereby conferred. The types of export incentives provided

---

[3] Collins-Williams and Salembier (1996) and Hoda and Ahuja (2005: 1009–1030) provide comprehensive explanation of the UR Subsidies Code, although they do not focus on export promotion policies.

by the government, but not regarded as subsidies, include the provision of general infrastructure such as railways, highways, ports and telecommunication lines. (Adamantopoulos, 2008: 436). Article 3.1 of the Subsidies Code prohibits: (a) export subsidies, which are provided contingent upon export performance and (b) import substituting subsidies, which are provided contingent upon the use of domestic over imported goods. The prohibition of export subsidies thus stipulated is not applied to the developing countries with a GNP per capita of less than US$1,000 per annum (Annex VII of the Subsidies Code), the LDCs hereafter. The Subsidies Code provides the Illustrative List of export subsidies prohibited, which includes 12 types of export subsidies.

Export subsidies appearing in the Illustrative List comprise, among others, the provision by governments of direct subsidies to a firm or an industry contingent upon export performance; currency retention schemes; internal transport and freight charges on export shipments, provided by governments, on terms more favourable than for domestic shipments; the provision by governments of imported or domestic products or services for the production of exported goods, on favourable terms; and the allowance of special deductions directly related to exports, over and above those granted with respect to production for domestic consumption. One interesting aspect of the Illustrative List of export subsidies is related to tax. According to the Illustrative List of export subsidies, the exemption or remission of direct tax is regarded as an export subsidy, although that of indirect tax such as VAT is not regarded as a subsidy (footnote 1 of the Subsidies Code).

The list also shows two examples that are specific to exports, i.e. duty drawback and an export insurance/credit scheme. Item (i) of the Illustrative List of export subsidies stipulates that the remission or drawback of import charges in excess of those levied on imported inputs that are consumed in the production of the exported product would be regarded as export subsidy. It implies that the amount of duty drawback not exceeding the threshold amount would not be regarded as export subsidies. Besides physically incorporated inputs, energy, fuels and oil used in the production process, and catalysts, which are consumed in the course of their use to produce the exported product, are regarded as inputs used in the production process. Meanwhile, capital goods are not regarded as being used in the production process even in case of depreciation (Hoda and Ahuja, 2005: 1015).

According to item (j) of the Illustrative List, the provision by governments or special institutions controlled by governments of export insurance programmes, of insurance against increases in the cost of exported products at premium rates which are inadequate to cover the long-term operating costs and losses of the programmes, is regarded as a type of export subsidy. Item (k) of the Illustrative List stipulates that if a member abides by the conditions in the OECD Arrangement

on Official Export Credits, then such export credits would not be regarded as
export subsidy.[4]

One interesting aspect of prohibition of export subsidy is that exchange rate
manipulation by the government benefiting exporters, i.e. devaluation or depreciation of domestic currency, is not regulated under the WTO regulations, although
it has a positive effect on export promotion like tax or financial incentives.
Meanwhile, there would be a limit on using it in the sense that devaluation or
depreciation of domestic currency would tend to have an inflationary effect that
the policy authorities generally wish to avoid.

Article 27 of the UR Subsidies Code deals with the SDT of developing countries. Among others, it recognises the important role of subsidies in the economic
development of developing countries, stipulating that

> Members recognize that subsidies may play an important role in economic development
> programmes of developing country Members. (Art. 27.1)

It also stipulates that prohibition of export promotion policies is not applied to
the LDCs without any specified time limit and other developing countries until
the end of 2002. Meanwhile, according to Article 27.5, an LDC that has reached
export competitiveness in any given product should phase out its export subsidies
over a period of eight years. Because the word 'export competitiveness' can be
interpreted arbitrarily, Article 27.6 provides the concrete criterion. That is, export
competitiveness in a product is considered to exist if a developing country's
exports of that product reach a share of at least 3.25 per cent in world trade of
that product for two consecutive calendar years. For the purposes of the export
competitiveness provision, a product is actually defined as a section of the har-
monized system (HS; Hoda and Ahuja, 2005: 1028).

Developing countries may also benefit from an SDT relating to *de minimis*
values. That is, any CVD investigation of a product imported from a developing
country should be terminated if (a) the overall level of subsidies granted upon the
product in question does not exceed 2 per cent of its value calculated on a per unit
basis, while the threshold is 1 per cent for developed countries, or (b) the volume
of the subsidised imports represents less than 4 per cent of the total imports of the
like product in the importing member (Art. 27.10). The favourable treatment of
developing countries in Article 27.10(b) is weakened by the cumulation provision
also appearing in it. That is, even if the imports from developing countries represent less than 4 per cent of the total imports of the like product in the importing
Member, if such imports collectively account for more than 9 per cent of the total

---

[4] Even in the 1970s, certain export incentives were regarded as such common practices that it would
be perhaps disruptive to apply CVDs against them. Export credit was one of such practices. In 1976,
the OECD Arrangement established guidelines for down payment amounts, interest rates and repay-
ment terms, which aimed at a closer approximation of the commercial market (Barcelo, 1977).

imports of the like product in the importing country, then the national authorities of the importing country can investigate the CVD.

Despite the existence of SDT provisions in the Subsidies Code of the WTO as is the case in the other agreements, the inclusion of such provisions might be dominated by the basic direction of the UR, which took the 'single undertaking' principle obliging all members to abide by basically all agreements in the WTO, irrespective of the economic development level. That is, up until the settlement of the UR, the contracting parties to the GATT 1947 could choose not to join the agreements. Most developing countries decided not to adhere to the NTB Codes in the Tokyo Round. Furthermore, many developing countries feel that the rules established as a result of the UR codify existing rules or practices created in the developed countries and do not reflect developing countries' needs (Wolfe, 2004: 588). Export insurances/credits can be mentioned as one of such practices.

3. WTO MEMBERS' POSITION ON EXPORT PROMOTION IN THE DDA

The Doha Ministerial Conference in November 2001 gave birth to the DDA negotiations. The Doha Ministerial Declaration emphasised the needs and interests of developing countries at the heart of those.[5] Thus, the WTO Members noticed that 'balanced rules' have important roles in the global trading system, although what is 'balanced' remains unclear. It reaffirmed that provisions for SDT are an integral part of the WTO Agreements,[6] although concrete details relating to SDT did not appear in the Declaration. Regarding subsidies, the Declaration called for

negotiations aimed at clarifying and improving disciplines under the Agreement(s) on Subsidies and Countervailing Measures . . . *taking into account the needs of developing and least-developed participants* (emphasis added by the author).[7]

In the same month of 2001, the Committee on Subsidies and Countervailing Measures of the WTO decided that prohibition of export subsidies provided by developing countries beginning from 2003 can be extended to the end of 2007, subject to annual reviews.[8] Such extension of the transition period lapsed.

The Hong Kong Ministerial Conference in December 2005 reaffirmed that the provisions for SDT are an integral part of the WTO Agreements and all SDT provisions should be reviewed with a view to strengthening them and making them more precise, effective and operational.[9] More concretely, it reaffirmed the SDT of products imported from the LDCs, saying that developed countries and devel-

---

[5] WTO, 'Doha Ministerial Declaration', 14 November 2001, para. 2.
[6] WTO, 'Doha Ministerial Declaration', 14 November 2001, para. 44.
[7] WTO, 'Doha Ministerial Declaration', 14 November 2001, para. 28.
[8] WTO, G/SCM/39, 'Procedures for extensions under Article 27.4 for certain developing country members', 20 November 2001, para. 1.(e).
[9] WTO, 'Hong Kong Ministerial Declaration', 18 December 2005, para. 35.

oping country Members declaring themselves in a position to do so agree to implement duty-free and quota-free market access for products originating from the LDCs. It also reaffirmed its support relating to trade-related technical assistance and capacity building to the LDCs on a priority basis in helping to overcome their limited human and institutional trade-related capacity.[10]

Duty-free and quota-free imports from the LDCs can be evaluated as a meaningful SDT. The Hong Kong Ministerial Declaration mentions the necessity of aid to build trade-related infrastructure, saying that aid for trade should aim to help developing countries, particularly the LDCs, to build the supply-side capacity and trade-related infrastructure.[11] Besides the duty-free and quota-free imports from the LDCs and support of institution building in those countries, there is no mention on the SDT of developing countries in general. Furthermore, there is no mention on the benefits of and/or preferential treatment of export promotion policies taken by developing countries. Instead of dealing with preferential treatment of export subsidies provided by developing countries, discussions in the development group at the Hong Kong Ministerial Conference centred on market access issues (Wilkinson, 2006: 298). Although the Hong Kong Ministerial Declaration did not mention the modification of the rules relating to export promotion policies of developing countries, several developing country members of the WTO actively argued for modification of the current rules in the WTO more in favour of policies leading to export expansion of those countries.

There have been proposals on modifying the rules on subsidies and CVDs during the DDA negotiations. Magnus (2004: 989) complains that those tabled are overwhelmingly weighted towards loosening direct disciplines on subsidies and/ or making it harder to use the CVD remedy. Meanwhile, such a complaint does not actually consider the development needs of developing countries, especially the beneficial role of export promotion by the government in some cases. In the DDA negotiations process, the WTO Members' views, with respect to export promotion of developing countries, have been significantly divided. India has led the developing countries' opinion and suggested many concrete ways of modifying the current regulations in favour of developing countries' export-led economic growth. It emphasised that the SDT provisions are meant to ensure that equal rules do not apply to unequal players.[12] It also noted disadvantages faced by industries in developing countries as compared to their counterparts in developed countries.[13] More specifically, it says that:

> industry in developing countries is characterized by low level of infrastructure development, high cost of capital, prevalence of underdeveloped regions where industries may be reluctant

---

[10] WTO, 'Hong Kong Ministerial Declaration', 18 December 2005, para. 47.
[11] WTO, 'Hong Kong Ministerial Declaration', 18 December 2005, para. 57.
[12] WTO, TN/RL/W/68, 'Communication from India', 11 March 2003, p. 1.
[13] WTO, TN/RL/W/4, 'Submission by India', 25 April 2002, p. 1.

to invest etc. The various export incentive schemes in developing countries are . . . more for the purpose of creating a level playing field, in view of the fact that their competitors from the developed countries do not suffer from these disadvantages.[14]

India suggested that a developing country has to assume a more active and positive role in assisting the industry by creating a level playing field[15] and providing the 'temporary' measure of SDT would not be appropriate for the developing countries facing 'structural' disadvantages.[16] Criticising the position of United States, India noticed that trade distortions made by export credits and agricultural subsidies which are in favour of developed countries are overlooked by developed countries.[17]

Meanwhile, the United States is adamant about not considering further SDT provision, saying that the objective of the Rules Group must be the continuation of the progressive strengthening and expansion of disciplines.[18] The United States reaffirmed its position, saying that the substance of the WTO prohibition on export subsidies and import substitution subsidies, and the general obligation of all members to eliminate such subsidies should be preserved.[19] Among developed countries, Canada appears to sympathise with the position of developing countries, especially small ones, in the sense of recognising that:

Recent dispute settlement decisions or factors relevant to the assessment of contingency on export performance have placed certain economies at an apparent disadvantage vis-à-vis those with large domestic markets.[20]

The WTO members' viewpoints on specific provisions are extremely divided with respect to Article 3 on prohibited subsidy. A radical view was suggested by Venezuela that all subsidies bestowed by developing countries should be treated as non-actionable subsidies.[21] However, the United States considered it to be appropriate to explore ways of strengthening the remedies for prohibited subsidies.[22]

Although the United States is opposed to loosening the Subsidies Code in general, it recognises the severe difficulties of the small, poorest countries, saying that for certain developing countries, not included in the LDCs in Annex VII, but whose economies were small and who had very small export shares of world trade, the transition period for export subsidy programmes can be extended.[23]

---

[14] WTO, TN/RL/W/68, 'Communication from India', 11 March 2003, p. 2.
[15] WTO, TN/RL/W/68, 'Communication from India', 11 March 2003, p. 2.
[16] WTO, TN/RL/W/40, 'Communication from India', 10 December 2002, p. 2.
[17] WTO, TN/RL/W/68, 'Communication from India', 11 March 2003, p. 3.
[18] WTO, TN/RL/W/27, 'Communication from the United States', 22 October 2002, p. 4.
[19] WTO, TN/RL/W/33, 'Communication from the United States', 2 December 2002, p. 4.
[20] WTO, TN/RL/W/1, 'Communication from Canada', 15 April 2002.
[21] WTO, TN/RL/W/41, 'Proposal by Venezuela', 17 December 2002, p. 2.
[22] WTO, TN/RL/W/78, 'Communication from the United States', 19 March 2003, p. 2.
[23] WTO, TN/RL/W/33, 'Communication from the United States', 2 December 2002, p. 2.

Among developed countries, the EC wants to establish clear and consistent rules for all types of export financing. The EC expresses sympathy with the developing countries' position with respect to the export credits and its preparedness to address the concerns of developing countries in this regard.[24] Brazil and India complain about the dominance of developed countries in using export credits. India declared that a grant of official export credits by OECD countries has been permitted, while most of the other countries have been prohibited from giving such credits[25] and opined that unreasonable benchmark premium rates have been used by developed countries.[26] Regarding item (k) of the Illustrative List, India proposed to change it into one where export credits are not supplied at rates below market rates.[27] Brazil complained that all participants of the OECD Arrangement are the OECD members and developing countries do not participate in the discussions and decisions in it. Brazil emphasised that under no circumstances should a small group of WTO members be allowed to change the rules through decisions taken in another forum, actually meaning the OECD.[28]

As average tariff rates of developing countries are generally high, there is much room for using duty drawback as an effective method of export promotion. India suggested that the current rules should be modified by making it more difficult to impose CVDs to duty drawback schemes.[29] It is India's view that in cases where over-rebate is found, the CVD must be limited to the extent of over-rebate. India also proposed that imported capital goods and consumables used in the production process should be included in the list of goods that are consumed in that relating to duty drawback.[30] Regarding duty drawback with respect to capital goods, India says that:

> developing countries have to impose customs duty on capital goods for meeting the exigencies of revenue generation. However they are not able to avail remission, exemption or deferral of such duties when the capital goods are used for production of products which are exported. Thus a level playing field is denied to the developing countries' exports as an element of customs duty paid on capital goods used get reflected in the total cost of the exported products. On the other hand, developed countries' exports do not include such costs as the customs duty on capital goods is low or the capital goods are manufactured within their countries.[31]

The Subsidies Code permits remission, exemption and deferral of prior stage cumulative indirect taxes on goods and services used in the production of exported

---

[24] WTO, TN/RL/W/30, 'Proposal by the European Communities', 21 November 2002, p. 4.
[25] WTO, TN/RL/W/68, 'Communication from India', 11 March 2003, p. 2.
[26] WTO, TN/RL/W/120, 'Communication from India', 16 June 2003, p. 3.
[27] WTO, TN/RL/W/177, 'Paper from Brazil', 31 March 2005, p. 3.
[28] WTO, TN/RL/W/177, 'Paper from Brazil', 31 March 2005, p. 1.
[29] WTO, TN/RL/W/120, 'Communication from India', 16 June 2003, pp. 1–3.
[30] WTO, TN/RL/W/120, 'Communication from India', 16 June 2003, p. 2.
[31] WTO, TN/RL/W/68, 'Communication from India', 11 March 2003, p. 2.

products. Meanwhile, India noticed the widespread lack of VAT system in developing countries.[32]

Among developed countries, without any concrete details, Canada took the attitude toward considering the reintroduction of nonactionable subsidies relating to Article 8.[33] The EC states the need to address the environmental dimension of subsidies following the expiry of Article 8 of the Subsidies Code.[34] India was worried about the EC's proposal in the sense that developing countries are not the main users of such subsidies because of the financial constraints.[35] In this sense, India expressed its position opposed to reintroducing nonactionable subsidies in lieu of Article 8 of the Subsidies Code.

Cuba and Venezuela focused on the fact that the document on Implementation-Related Issues and Concerns set out four legitimate development goals, i.e. regional growth, technology research and development, production diversification and implementation of environmentally sound methods of production. Cuba and Venezuela proposed that the WTO system might treat measures taken in pursuit of any one of these goals as nonactionable if adopted by developing countries.[36] These four legitimate development goals comprise three types of subsidies illustrated in Article 8 and an additional type relating to product diversification, which can be interpreted as one from specialisation in primary products to industrialisation. Of these four development goals, Cuba and Venezuela regard diversification of production as having key importance and a topmost priority in a country's development policy.[37]

Even the United States, which appears to be one of the least sympathetic to developing countries in export subsidies issue, admits the difficulties faced by developing countries with respect to the notification requirements, saying that consideration should be given to other ways of lessening the burden on those, especially the LDCs.[38] Such an approach by the United States with respect to notification appears to be due to its recognition that the resource of government officials in small developing countries that can deal with such notification requirements is very limited.

Regarding Article 27.5 and 27.6 of the Subsidies Code, India says that there should be a discussion on the provision that a developing country (LDC) that has reached 3.25 per cent in world trade of a product for two consecutive calendar years should phase out its export subsidies over two (eight)-year periods.[39] India's

---

[32] WTO, TN/RL/W/120, 'Communication from India', 16 June 2003, p. 2.

[33] WTO, TN/RL/W/1, 'Communication from Canada', 15 April 2002.

[34] WTO, TN/RL/W/30, 'Proposal by the European Communities', 21 November 2002.

[35] WTO, TN/RL/W/40, 'Communication from India', 10 December 2002, pp. 1–2.

[36] WTO, TN/RL/W/131, 'Communication from Cuba and Venezuela', 11 July 2003, p. 1.

[37] WTO, TN/RL/W/131, 'Communication from Cuba and Venezuela', 11 July 2003, p. 4.

[38] WTO, TN/RL/W/78, 'Communication from the United States', 19 March 2003.

[39] WTO, TN/RL/W/120, 'Communication from India', 16 June 2003, p. 3.

proposal reflects the viewpoint of a large, developing country whose share in a product may be bigger than 3.25 per cent. For the SDT provision, India proposed that CVDs should not be imposed in the case of imports from developing countries where the total volume of imports is negligible, i.e. 7 per cent of total imports. Regarding *de minimis* subsidy, India also proposed that export subsidies granted by developing countries where they account for less than 5 per cent of the f.o.b. value of the product should be treated as nonactionable.[40]

Of developed countries, the EC expressed that it is ready to sign off on additional derogations – going beyond the set already provided in Art. 27 of the Subsidies Code for developing countries under the heading of the SDT.[41] As, unlike the Antidumping Code, the Subsidies Code does not contain any requirement that the 'special situation' of developing countries should be taken into account when taking CVDs (Avgoustidi and Ballschmiede, 2008: 725), the EC proposed that it is necessary to consider the incorporation of such provisions into Article 27 of the Subsidies Code.[42] Meanwhile, the EC has not provided further concrete details on the additional derogation.

The Draft Chair Text of the Negotiating Group on Rules of the WTO, which was released in December 2008, includes the following changes that are related to the export promotion concerns of developing countries.[43] Regarding Article 3 on prohibited subsidies, except for a provision prohibiting fisheries subsidies that contribute to overcapacity and overfishing, there is no change. On the Illustrative List of export subsidies appearing in Annex I, there is no change in either the provision on direct and indirect taxes or that on the duty drawback scheme. That is to say, India's suggestions on those issues are not reflected at all in the Draft Chair Text. Meanwhile, it mentions that there is no consensus on the 'cost-to-government' versus 'benefit-to-recipient' criterion in deciding subsidy relating to export credit, guarantee or insurance in item (j). It also mentions that there is no consensus on the provision acknowledging the OECD Arrangement, which reflects a few developing countries' criticism with respect to item (k).

Regarding the criterion of the LDCs' exemption from prohibition of export subsidies, the Draft Text modifies the relevant provision in Annex VII into

In constant 1990 dollars for three consecutive years . . . and (a) Member . . . shall be reincluded in the list in Annex VII(b) when its GNP per capita falls back below US$1,000.[44]

---

[40] WTO, TN/RL/W/4, 'Submission by India', 25 April 2002, p. 2.
[41] WTO, TN/RL/W/30, 'Proposal by the European Communities', 21 November 2002.
[42] WTO, TN/RL/GEN/93, 'Countervailing Measures: Paper from the European Communities', 18 November 2005, p. 4.
[43] WTO, TN/RL/W/236, 'New Draft Consolidated Chair Texts of the AD and SCM Agreements', 19 December 2008.
[44] WTO, TN/RL/W/68, 'Communication from India', 11 March 2003, p. 2.

On Article 27 relating to SDT, any proposal made by a developing country is not reflected except for export competitiveness. For export competitiveness, the Draft Text mentions the split in the opinions of the members, saying that views differ considerably among the members as to the best way to do this, including changing the period and/or methodology for calculating the share of world trade in a product, or clarifying the definition of a 'product' for this purpose. It also says that views differ widely as to whether the reintroduction of export subsidies should be allowed if export competitiveness is lost after having been reached, and, if so, on what basis and for how long.[45]

It is noteworthy that there is no modification of the SDT provision at all in the Draft Text despite many proposals by developing countries. Neither is there any change in Art. 31 on provisional application, meaning that the nonactionable subsidies appearing in Article 8 are no longer nonactionable, according to the 2008 Draft Text.[46]

4. MODIFICATION OF THE EXPORT PROMOTION PROVISIONS
IN THE SUBSIDIES CODE

a. Nonreciprocity as Distributional Fairness

Supporters of trade liberalisation such as Srinivasan (1999) argue that it would be beneficial for developing countries to participate fully in the liberal world trading system. Finger and Winters (1998) even suggest that SDT provisions in the global trading system led to the delay in integrating the developing countries into the world economy. Meanwhile, regarding export promotion, their argument is inconsistent with the experience of the developing countries that grew very fast during past decades. Even if developing countries wish to pursue export promotion policies, many instruments that the rapidly growing economies such as South Korea and Taiwan utilised in their export-led economic growth process are not allowed in the current WTO system. Therefore, it is necessary for developing countries to think of concrete ideas and put pressures on modifying the current WTO regulations in favour of promoting their exports, which, of course, can be justified from the viewpoint of 'fairness' in international trade.

Regarding fairness in international trade, we can contrast 'non-discrimination fairness' with 'distributional fairness'. The former can be defined by assuming that there is a set of groups deemed to be equal. From the viewpoint of 'nondiscrimination fairness', if one of these groups is allowed to take some action, then

---

[45] WTO, TN/RL/W/68, 'Communication from India', 11 March 2003, p. 2.
[46] WTO, TN/RL/W/68, 'Communication from India', 11 March 2003, p. 2.

all other groups should also be allowed to take the same action (Suranovic, 2000: 288). The basic principles of the GATT/WTO, i.e. national treatment and most-favoured nation (MFN) treatment, follow the 'non-discrimination fairness'. 'Distributional fairness' can be defined as equality fairness applied to final outcomes or attributes. It is based on a belief that the distributions of benefits among individuals, after all actions are taken, would need to be equalised to be fair in distribution (Suranovic, 2000: 290–291).[47] SDT of developing countries in the GATT/WTO can be understood in terms of 'distributional fairness' applied to international trade relations, which aim to narrow the gap between developed countries and developing countries with respect to per capita income.

As Wade (2003) argues, nonreciprocity between developed and developing countries in favour of the latter needs to be strengthened because of the different levels of economic development between these two groups.[48] Although current trade regulations generally limit government intervention in international trade compared with the previous GATT, according to Weiss (2005: 744), for developed countries, the disciplinary effect of multilateral trade rules has been government augmenting, offering generous room to manoeuvre in areas such as technology development. It would be opposite to the direction of 'distributional fairness'.

Developing countries may promote export if more market access opportunities are given from their trade partners, most of whom are developed countries, and their supply capacities are expanded (Wolfe, 2004: 584). Explaining the case of sub-Saharan African (SSA) countries, Blackhurst et al. (2000) explain that most if not all SSA governments, especially technocrats and the private sectors in those countries, now accept that the key problem at this point in time after the UR is not a lack of market access opportunities, but rather the inadequate domestic supply response to existing market access opportunities. Therefore, it would be more appropriate for the WTO Members to think of ways of promoting export capacities of developing countries and alleviating the threat of trade remedies such as CVDs against the products exported from developing countries.

b. Modifying the Subsidies Code

Many current provisions in the WTO acknowledge the special situation of developing countries. Regarding a trade dispute in the WTO system, it was made clear that there will always be justification for claiming that a given subsidy is not

---

[47] A belief in egalitarianism is the case that distributional fairness is applied in the extreme. Although pure egalitarianism is rarely suggested any longer, less stringent applications of egalitarianism still remain, such as a belief that a more equal distribution of income and/or wealth is preferable to a less equal distribution (Suranovic, 2000: 290).
[48] Similarly, Qureshi (2003: 869) proposed that non-reciprocity principle appearing in GATT Article XXXVI(8) should be mirrored in the interpretation process of the WTO Agreements, i.e. the dispute settlement panels in the WTO regarding disputes between developing and developed members.

inconsistent with 'development needs' (Benitah, 2001: 186). Whether a measure reflects those would depend on the decision of the concerned government. From the viewpoint of distributional fairness, it may be necessary for the future WTO system to start from incorporating the phrase 'development needs' of developing countries in the SDT provision of the Subsidies Code.

Article 6.1 of the Subsidies Code stipulates the criteria of the existence of serious prejudice. One of those is 'the total ad valorem subsidisation of a product exceeding 5 per cent'. It lapsed at the end of 1999. As an SDT of developing countries, it may be conceivable to make the paragraph concerned effective with respect to developing countries and combine it with modification of *de minimis* subsidy provision. Then, if the products exported by the developing countries are subsidised below the threshold level, they would not be subject to imposition of CVDs.

The R&D subsidy that was categorised as nonagricultural subsidy until the end of 1999 is currently not nonactionable. The current negotiations in the WTO about rules have so far seen limited discussion on the possible reintroduction of a category of nonactionable subsidies (Rios Herran and Poretti, 2008: 749). R&D is usually regarded as having positive externality. Therefore, compared with resource allocation without government intervention, from the welfare viewpoint, it would be better to provide an R&D subsidy. Without it, there would be underproduction of R&D. In addition, if we look at the evidence of the north-east Asian dynamic economies, R&D policy and the consequent development of technology intensive industries have contributed significantly to the economic development of those, for instance.[49] It would be necessary to think of considering the SDT of categorising the R&D subsidy provided by developing countries as nonactionable, partly reflecting the proposal by Cuba and Venezuela.[50]

Developing countries are likely to be subjected to the imposition of CVDs but are less likely to have the resource to investigate foreign subsidies negatively affecting their economies (Horlick and Shoop, 2008: 694). Therefore, even besides the issue of pursuing their own export promotion policies and economic development, developing countries are at a disadvantage with respect to CVDs.

The current Subsidies Code allows the national authorities to be able to cumulatively assess import volume in investigating material injury to domestic producers. Therefore, cumulation has become a common practice in investigating the CVD cases (Durling, 2008: 607). To control abuse of CVDs, it would be necessary to eliminate the cumulation provision appearing in Article 15.3 of the Subsidies Code.

Article 27 of the Subsides Code acknowledges the important role of subsidies in economic development, and thereby, the LDCs are allowed to grant export

---

[49] See Ahn and Mah (2007) for Korea and Kim and Mah (2009) for China for details.
[50] WTO, TN/RL/W/131, 'Communication from Cuba and Venezuela', 11 July 2003.

subsidies. Although it may make room for the LDCs' use of export subsidies, as developed countries can offset the effect of provision of export subsidies by CVDs, such preferential treatment of the LDCs may become meaningless. Therefore, it would be conceivable for developed countries not to impose CVDs against the products that were provided export subsidies by the LDCs,[51] if they do not exceed, for instance, 10 or 15 per cent *ad valorem*.[52] A somewhat lower threshold level can be similarly introduced at the same time.

As it is not likely that small developing country products are exported to developed countries for predatory purposes, it would not be appropriate to prohibit export subsidies provided by small developing countries. In addition, export subsidies may be needed if they should earn foreign exchange to relieve themselves of the serious balance of payments difficulties. They often face such a situation because of the fact that most developing countries have suffered from continuing current account deficits. It may be worthwhile to design a provision not imposing CVDs against developing countries undergoing chronic current account deficits.

Furthermore, we can think of modifying the current provision on the prohibition of export subsidies into not prohibiting export subsidies by developing countries in general. Then, the subsidised products may be subject to the imposition of CVDs by the importing country. It is not so likely that the exports of small developing countries subsidised by their governments result in material injury to the concerned industry in developed countries. Therefore, they may not be subjected to the imposition of CVDs by developed countries. Alternatively, we may think of applying the 'export competitiveness' criterion with respect to developing countries in general if developed countries are worried about losing competitiveness to the large developing countries. Then, the preferential treatment can be restricted to small developing economies.

In Article 27.2 of the Subsidies Code, as is the case in the other agreements, the transition period for developing countries was set too short, as economic development is a long process.[53] Consequently, it would be necessary to reintroduce and lengthen the transition period to, say, 20–25 years on the condition that

---

[51] In the context of industrial policies of developing countries, Lee (2004) proposed trade protection measures comprising import substituting tariff, not prohibiting developing countries as a whole using export subsidies, and not putting limitations on CVD actions against imports from developing countries, allowing subsidies provided by developing countries depending on the percentages of their exports in total trade values.

[52] The suggested threshold level reflects the fact that South Korea's and Taiwan's export subsidy ratios were about or higher than 11–13 per cent during the active export promotion period.

[53] Pangetsu (2000: 1293) also noticed the unrealistic transition period with respect to the other Agreements such as the Agreement on Trade-related Aspects of Intellectual Property Rights (TRIPs) and Customs Valuation Agreement given the limited resources of developing countries needed to set up new institutions, regulatory framework, physical infrastructure and training of human resources. Therefore, Bora et al. (2000: 556–57) suggested an extension of the transition period relating to industrial policy.

the developing country concerned does not reach developed country status during the relevant period. Although such a treatment of export subsidies may appear to be too generous to developing countries, by invoking Article 27.5 and 27.6 of the Subsidies Code, i.e. the 'export competitiveness' provision, the WTO system can control the trade-distorting effect of the use of export subsidies.

For export credit and export insurance, it would be appropriate to discuss the conditions such as the benchmark fee level not in the forum monopolised by developed countries such as the OECD, as Brazil suggested.[54] Regarding indirect tax such as VAT, although it is true that many developing countries do not yet have such schemes, they have recently introduced or are taking steps to introduce them. Therefore, unlike India's proposal, the current provision allowing VAT exemption to exported products would be appropriate. For duty drawback with respect to depreciation of capital goods used in the process of producing exported goods, although India's proposal explained in Section 3 makes sense qualitatively, it may be too difficult to arrive at a consensus on the method of calculating it quantitatively. Because even most developed countries understand the administrative difficulties of small developing countries with respect to the notification requirement, it would not be difficult to modify Article 25 on notification requirement in favour of small developing countries.[55]

5. CONCLUSIONS

Some critics of the WTO system have argued that most policy options except for human capital policies such as education and training have been prohibited (Held et al., 1999: 187–88). They also argue that the measures permitted are developed country friendly and such allowed measures enable the developed countries to align their national economic development goals with support for industry, technology and exports (Weiss, 2005: 724). Such arguments can be regarded as an exaggeration of the characteristics of the current WTO regulations in the sense of the existence of SDT provisions in the UR Subsidies Code. Meanwhile, it is true that the Subsidies Code has made less room for export promotion policies of developing countries than the situation before the operation of the WTO regulations.

It would be possible for the current developing country members of the WTO to utilise available export promotion measures and existing SDT provisions in the WTO. Even the developed countries actively utilise export promotion measures such as export finance/insurance which are not prohibited in the current Subsidies Code, realising the benefits of export expansion. Although it is true that the

---

[54] WTO, TN/RL/W/177, 'Paper from Brazil', 31 March 2005, p. 1.
[55] For further details on modification of the Subsidies Code, see Mah (2010: 887–90).

current WTO system prohibits export subsidies and strictly regulates the provision of subsidies by allowing the imposition of CVDs, developing countries, especially the LDCs, can still provide subsidies to promote exports. The LDCs can provide export subsidies to promote exports as long as their share falls short of the export competitiveness threshold level. Although they may be subject to the imposition of CVDs, the share of such imports from small developing economies in particular would be likely to be insignificant and it would be difficult for the investigating authorities to prove the existence of material injury to their domestic producers.

Developing economies may also provide a small number of export subsidies up to the stipulated *de minimis* level, i.e. 2 per cent of product values for developing countries. Even large developing economies can provide such a *de minimis* number of subsidies, which is not actionable. Meanwhile, such a small amount of subsidy may not be so effective in promoting exports, if we think of the high subsidy ratios of the north-east Asian developing economies during the active export promotion period.

Realising the limited availability of export promotion measures, certain developing countries proposed the ideas of SDT with respect to export promotion policies in the DDA negotiation process. After explaining such developing country Members' proposals, the current paper suggests various ways of modifying the current UR Subsidies Code in favour of the export promotion of developing countries. Such SDT based on nonreciprocity can be justified from the viewpoint of 'distributional fairness', as there exist extreme differences in economic development levels between developed and developing countries.

Limiting full developing countries' participation and the consequent dissatisfaction of developing countries regarding the extent to which their interests were reflected could be regarded as an important cause of the failures of the WTO Ministerial Conferences. Therefore, the success of future WTO negotiations will be imperilled without greater balance between developed and developing countries (Stiglitz, 2000: 437; Wolfe, 2004: 580). Maintaining and improving the WTO system has been more unlikely without further SDT consideration of developing countries. Making more room for developing countries to move with respect to export promotion is expected to contribute to export-led growth of developing countries and, subsequently, stability of the world economy.

REFERENCES

Adamantopoulos, K. (2008), 'Article 1 SCMA', in W. Rudiger, P. T. Stoll and M. Koebele (eds.), *WTO – Trade Remedies* (Leiden and Boston: Martinus Nijhoff Publishers), 423–52.
Adamantopoulos, K. and V. Akritidis (2008), 'Article 3 SCMA', in W. Rudiger, P. T. Stoll and M. Koebele (eds.), *WTO – Trade Remedies* (Leiden and Boston, MA: Martinus Nijhoff Publishers), 471–86.

Ahn, H. J. and J. S. Mah (2007), 'Development of Technology Intensive Industries in Korea', *Journal of Contemporary Asia*, **37**, 3, 364–79.

Avgoustidi, V. and S. Ballschmiede (2008), 'Article 27 SCMA', in W. Rudiger, P. T. Stoll and M. Koebele (eds.), *WTO – Trade Remedies* (Leiden and Boston, MA: Martinus Nijhoff Publishers), 702–25.

Barcelo, J. J. (1977), 'Subsidies and Countervailing Duties – Analysis and a Proposal', *Law and Policy in International Business*, **9**, 3, 779–852.

Benitah, M. (2001), *The Law of Subsidies Under the GATT/WTO System* (London: Kluwer Law International).

Blackhurst, R., B. Lyakurwa and A. Oyejide (2000), 'Options for Improving Africa's Participation in the WTO', *The World Economy*, **23**, 4, 491–510.

Bora, B., P. J. Loyd and M. Pangetsu (2000), 'Industrial Policy and the WTO', *The World Economy*, **23**, 4, 543–59.

Brander, J. A. and B. J. Spencer (1985), 'Export Subsidies and International Market Share Rivalry', *Journal of International Economics*, **18**, 1/2, 83–100.

Collins-Williams, T. and G. Salembier (1996), 'International Disciplines on Subsidies: The GATT, the WTO and the Future Agenda', *Journal of World Trade*, **30**, 1, 5–17.

Durling, J. P. (2008), 'Article 15 SCMA', in W. Rudiger, P. T. Stoll and M. Koebele (eds.), *WTO – Trade Remedies* (Leiden and Boston, MA: Martinus Nijhoff Publishers), 598–626.

Falvey, R. E. and N. Gemmell (1990), 'Compensatory Financial and Fiscal Incentives to Exports', in C. Milner (ed.), *Export Promotion Strategies: Theory and Evidence from Developing Countries* (New York: Harvester Wheatsheaf), 109–29.

Finger, J. M. and L. A. Winters (1998), 'What Can the WTO Do for Developing Countries?' in A. O. Krueger (ed.), *The WTO as an International Organization* (Chicago, IL and London: University of Chicago Press).

Held, D., A. McGrew, D. Goldblatt and J. Pettaton (1999), *Global Transformations: Politics, Economics and Culture* (Cambridge: Polity Press).

Hoda, A. and R. Ahuja (2005), 'Agreement on Subsidies and Countervailing Measures: Need for Clarification and Improvement', *Journal of World Trade*, **39**, 6, 1009–69.

Horlick, G. N. and K. Shoop (2008), 'Article 25 SCMA', in Wolfrum, Rudiger, Peter Tobias Stoll and Michael Koebele (eds.), *WTO – Trade Remedies* (Leiden and Boston, MA: Martinus Nijhoff Publishers), 687–94.

Kim, M.-J. and J. S. Mah (2009), 'China's R&D Policies and Technology-Intensive Industries', *Journal of Contemporary Asia*, **39**, 2, 262–78.

Lee, Y.-S. (2004), 'Facilitating Development in the World Trading System – A Proposal for Development Facilitation Tariff and Development Facilitating Subsidy', *Journal of World Trade*, **38**, 6, 935–54.

Magnus, J. R. (2004), 'World Trade Organization Subsidy Discipline: Is This the "Retrenchment Round"?' *Journal of World Trade*, **38**, 6, 985–1047.

Mah, J. S. (2002), 'Regulatory Lessons from the South Korean Currency Crisis: Comment on Zalewski', *Journal of Economic Issues*, **36**, 3, 804–09.

Mah, J. S. (2008), 'The Role of Special Economic Zone in Economic Development: The Case of Shenzhen in China', *Journal of World Investment and Trade*, **9**, 4, 319–32.

Mah, J. S. (2010), 'Government-led Export Promotion in Light of Distributional Fairness in the Global Trading System', *Journal of Economic Issues*, **44**, 4, 877–94.

Mah, J. S. and C. Milner (2005), 'The Japanese Export Insurance Arrangements: Subsidisation or Promotion?' *The World Economy*, **28**, 2, 231–42.

Meyer, W. (1984), 'The Infant-Export Industry Argument', *Canadian Journal of Economics*, **17**, 249–69.

Milner, C. (ed.) (1990), *Export Promotion Strategies: Theory and Evidence from Developing Countries* (New York: Harvester Wheatsheaf).

Narlikar, A. (2006), 'Fairness in International Trade Negotiations: Developing Countries in the GATT and WTO', *The World Economy*, **29**, 8, 1005–29.

Pangetsu, M. (2000), 'Special and Differential Treatment in the Millennium: Special for Whom and How Different?' *The World Economy*, **23**, 9, 1285–302.

Qureshi, A. H. (2003), 'Interpreting World Trade Organization Agreements for the Development Objective', *Journal of World Trade*, **37**, 5, 847–82.

Rios Herran, R. and P. Poretti (2008), 'Article 31 SCMA', in W. Rudiger, P. T. Stoll and M. Koebele (eds.), *WTO – Trade Remedies* (Leiden and Boston, MA: Martinus Nijhoff Publishers), 747–49.

Seringhaus, F. H. R. and P. J. Rosson (1990), *Government Export Promotion: A Global Perspective* (London: Routledge).

Singer, H. W. (1988), 'The World Development Report 1987 on the Blessings of Outward Orientation: A Necessary Correction', *Journal of Development Studies*, **24**, 232–36.

Srinivasan, T. N. (1999), *Developing Countries and the Multilateral Trading System: From the GATT to the Uruguay Round and the Future* (Boulder, CO: Westview Press).

Stiglitz, J. E. (2000), 'Two Principles for the Next Round or, How to Bring Developing Countries in from the Cold', *The World Economy*, **23**, 4, 437–54.

Suranovic, S. M. (2000), 'A Positive Analysis of Fairness with Applications to International Trade', *The World Economy*, **23**, 3, 283–307.

Wade, R. H. (1991), 'How to Protect Exports from Protection: Taiwan's Duty Drawback Scheme', *The World Economy*, **14**, 3, 299–310.

Wade, R. H. (2003), 'What Strategies are Viable for Developing Countries Today? The World Trade Organization and the Shrinking of "Development Space"', *Review of International Political Economy*, **10**, 4, 621–44.

Wade, R. H. (2004), *Governing the Market*, 2nd edn (Princeton, NJ and Oxford: Princeton University Press).

Warr, P. (1990), 'Export Processing Zones', in C. Milner (ed.), *Export Promotion Strategies: Theory and Evidence from Developing Countries* (New York: Harvester Wheatsheaf), 130–61.

Weiss, L. (2005), 'Global Governance, National Strategies: How Industrialized States Make Room to Move Under the WTO', *Review of International Political Economy*, **12**, 5, 723–49.

Wilkinson, R. (2006), 'The WTO in Hong Kong: What It Really Means for the Doha Development Agenda', *New Political Economy*, **11**, 2, 291–303.

Wolfe, R. (2004), 'Crossing the River by Feeling the Stones: Where the WTO is Going After Seattle, Doha and Cancun', *Review of International Political Economy*, **11**, 3, 574–96.

Index

The World Economy: Global Trade Policy 2011, First Edition. Edited by David Greenaway.
Chapters © 2013 The Authors. Published © 2013 Blackwell Publishing Ltd.